With Set Work and Areas of Study
for examinations from 2009 to 2011

Paul Terry

YEOVIL COLLEGE

LIBRARY

Rhinegold Education

239–241 Shaftesbury Avenue
London WC2H 8TF
Telephone: 020 7333 1720
Fax: 020 7333 1765

www.rhinegold.co.uk

Rhinegold Music Study Guides
(series editor: Paul Terry)

GCSE, AS and A2 Music Study Guides for the AQA, Edexcel and OCR Specifications
Listening Tests for GCSE, AS and A2 Music for the AQA, Edexcel and OCR Specifications
GCSE Music Study Guide for the WJEC Specification
Music Technology Study Guide for the Edexcel AS and A2 Specification
Listening Tests for the AS and A2 Music Technology Edexcel Specification
Lifelines Revision Guides for GCSE, AS and A2 Music for the AQA and Edexcel Specifications
Lifelines Revision Guides for AS and A2 Music Technology for the Edexcel Specification
Understanding Harmony (AS) and Applied Harmony (A2)
Music Composition Workbook
Music Literacy Workbook

Also available from Rhinegold Education

Key Stage 3 Elements
Key Stage 3 Listening Tests: Book 1 and Book 2
Baroque Music in Focus, Romanticism in Focus, Modernism in Focus
Batman in Focus, *Goldfinger* in Focus, *Madonna* in Focus, *Who's Next* in Focus
Film Music in Focus, Musicals in Focus

Rhinegold Publishing also publishes Classical Music, Classroom Music, Early Music Today, Music Teacher,
Opera Now, Piano, The Singer, Teaching Drama, British and International Music Yearbook,
British Performing Arts Yearbook, British Music Education Yearbook, Rhinegold Dictionary of Music in Sound.

Other Rhinegold Study Guides

Rhinegold publishes resources for candidates studying Classical Civilisation, Drama and Theatre Studies,
Performance Studies and Religious Studies.

First published 2008 in Great Britain by
Rhinegold Publishing Limited
239–241 Shaftesbury Avenue
London WC2H 8TF
Telephone: 020 7333 1720
Fax: 020 7333 1765
www.rhinegold.co.uk

You should always check the current requirements of the examination, since these may change.
Copies of the AQA Specification can be downloaded from the AQA website at http://www.aqa.org.uk/ or
may be purchased from AQA Publications, Unit Two, Wheel Forge Way, Trafford Park, Manchester M17 1EH
Telephone 0870 410 1036   Fax 0161 953 1177   Email: publications@aqa.org.uk

AQA AS Music Study Guide (2009–2011)
British Library Cataloguing in Publication Data.
A catalogue record for this book is available from the British Library.
ISBN 978-1-906178-27-7
Printed in Great Britain by Headley Brothers Ltd

Contents

The details of the AS Music examination are believed to be correct at the time of going to press, but readers should always check the current requirements for the examination with AQA, since these may change. The AQA music specification is available at www.aqa.org.uk.

The author

Richard Knight read music at St John's College, Oxford, and has been director of music at two leading independent schools. He now combines teaching with work as a principal examiner at A level and is on the panel of examiners for the ABRSM. Richard is one of the authors of *Elements: The Rhinegold Guide to Key Stage 3 Music* and a frequent contributor to *Classroom Music*. He also presents conferences for students and teachers.

As a composer, he has a large catalogue of works to his name, including the oratorio *The Crown of Life*, a classroom musical *The King of Ireland's Son*, and various orchestral and chamber works. Richard has a particular interest in all things South American and is also an inland waterways enthusiast.

The editor

Paul Terry was director of music at the City of London Freemen's School for 15 years and later taught music at Kingston University. He has served as chief examiner in music for two A-level boards, and has written many textbooks on music and music technology. Paul is music series editor for the Rhinegold Study Guides.

Acknowledgements

The author and editor would like to thank the following members of the Rhinegold editorial team: Lucien Jenkins, Katherine Smith and Sam Queen.

The author and publishers are grateful to the following publishers for permission to use printed excerpts from their publications:

Do You Love Me?: Words by Sheldon Harnick and music by Jerry Bock. © 1964 Times Square Music Publications and Jerry Bock Enterprises Ltd. Carlin Music Corp. Reproduced by permission of Faber Music Ltd. All Rights Reserved.

Poor Professor Higgins: Words by Alan Lerner and music by Frederick Loewe. © 1964 Chappell Music Ltd. Chappell Morris Ltd. Reproduced by permission of Faber Music Ltd. All Rights Reserved.

Love Me Do: Words and music by John Lennon and Paul McCartney. © Copyright 1962 MPL Communications Limited. Used by permission of Music Sales Limited. All rights reserved. International copyright secured.

Sacrifice: Words and music by Elton John and Bernie Taupin. © Copyright 1989 HST Management Limited and Rouge Booze Incorporated (administered by Universal Music Publishing Limited). Used by permission of Music Sales Limited. All rights reserved. International copyright secured.

Underneath the Sky: Words and music by Noel Gallagher. © Copyright 1995 Oasis Music/Creation Songs Limited. Song/ATV Music Publishing (UK) Limited. Used by permission of Music Sales Limited. All rights reserved. International copyright secured.

The Scientist: Words and music by Guy Berryman, Chris Martin, Jon Buckland and Will Champion. © Copyright 2002 BMG Music Publishing Limited. Universal Music Publishing MGB Limited. Used by permission of Music Sales Limited. All rights reserved. International copyright secured.

Who Needs Love: Words and music by Johnny Borrell. © Copyright 2006 Sony/ATV Music Publishing (UK) Limited. Used by permission of Music Sales Limited. All rights reserved. International copyright secured.

Ghost Town by Jerry Dammers. © 1981 Plangent Visions Music Limited.

Somebody To Love: Words and music by Freddie Mercury. © 1976 Queen Music Ltd Reproduced by permission of International Music Publications Ltd (a trading name of Faber Music Ltd). All Rights Reserved.

Introduction

About the course

The AQA AS Music exam consists of three units:

1 **Influences on Music**
   A written paper, accounting for 30% of the marks

2 **Creating Musical Ideas**
   Composing coursework, accounting for 30% of the marks

3 **Interpreting Musical Ideas**
   Performing, accounting for 40% of the marks.

> AQA stands for the Assessment and Qualifications Alliance. It is the organisation that decides what you have to do in each part of this exam, supervises the marking, and awards grades and certificates.

Unit 1

For this paper you are required to:

➤ Listen to some excerpts of music, and then be tested on your aural perception and ability to understand some of the details of the music you hear

➤ Write an essay on a set work taken from the compulsory area of study, 'The Western Classical Tradition'. For the examinations in June 2009 to June 2011 the set work is:

   Mozart's Symphony No. 41 in C, K551 (movements 1 and 3)

> AQA have announced that the focus of this area of study and the set work may change every three years. The set work given here will be examined in June 2009, June 2010 and June 2011.

➤ Write an essay on a second area of study. For the examinations in June 2009 to June 2011 you can choose **one** of the following areas of study:

   Choral Music in the Baroque Period
   Music Theatre: A Study of the Musical from 1940 to 1980
   British Popular Music from 1960 to the Present Day.

There should be regular time given to studying the set work and material for the second area of study during the year. You will also need to have regular practice to train your aural skills. Your exam answers will be sent to an AQA examiner for marking.

Unit 2

Composing is done as coursework over a timed period of 20 hours, during which you have to complete **one** of the following briefs:

➤ Two exercises in compositional techniques

➤ A three- to six-minute composition in one of four set genres

➤ An arrangement of a set folksong melody for voices, instruments or ICT.

> In music, 'genre' refers to categories such as vocal music, keyboard music and so forth.

The specific briefs will be available for you from 1 November. There should be plenty of opportunity to develop your compositional skills before and after that date. Your completed coursework will be sent to an AQA examiner for marking by 15 May.

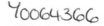

Unit 3

For this unit you have to submit recordings of your performances in **two** categories from the following list:

➢ A solo instrumental performance

➢ A solo vocal performance

➢ A solo instrumental performance on a second instrument

➢ An ensemble performance

➢ A performance through technology using sequencing

➢ A performance through technology using multi-tracked or close microphone recording.

The programme for each category should be 5–8 minutes in length and may consist of a single piece or a group of short pieces. Your performances will be marked by a teacher at your centre and sent to AQA by 15 May for moderation.

About this guide

This book will help you prepare for the exam by providing advice and exercises to improve your aural perception for the first section of Unit 1, a detailed analysis of the first and third movements of Mozart's *Jupiter* Symphony for the second section, and information about representative works for whichever area of study you choose for the third section of the unit.

There is also guidance on some of the techniques required for completing the briefs in Unit 2 and advice on preparing performances for Unit 3.

AS examinations are usually taken at the end of a single year's study. In practice this means your teacher has only about 24 weeks in which to prepare you and your fellow students. It is therefore a feature of AS that more onus for progress will fall on your own shoulders than was the case during the typical two years spent on GCSE music. Take the initiative, therefore, and use this book as the starting point for your own studies. You will then find that your teacher's input is all the more effective since it will build on what you have already found out for yourself.

AS music doesn't just examine your success at mastering a defined area of knowledge; it also tests your general musical skills through examining your aural perception, your creative imagination and your ability to communicate musical ideas through performing. Because of this you should, throughout the year, try to broaden your musical experience as much as you can: learn to play new pieces, take part in group activities, try improvising on your instrument regularly to create different moods, listen to as wide a range of music as you can, attend concerts if you have the chance.

All of this will help to inform your musical understanding and maximise your potential. It should also make your year of studying AS music highly enjoyable. Good luck!

Unit 1:
Influences on Music

For this unit you will have to take a written paper which lasts for 1¾ hours. It accounts for 30% of your AS mark. There will be three sections:

➤ Section A Listening (40 marks, approximately 30 minutes)

➤ Section B Historical Study: Area of Study 1 (20 marks)

➤ Section C Historical Study: Area of Study 2 (20 marks)

Section A requires listening to a recording of musical extracts on which questions are set. This is similar to the GCSE listening test. Once the recording has finished, the remainder of the exam will be conducted in normal exam conditions, so you will have the rest of the time to check your Section A answers and tackle the essay questions for Sections B and C. You will have to answer one essay from a choice of two for each of these sections.

Although you will spend longer in the exam on Sections B and C, each of these is marked out of 20, whereas Section A is marked out of 40. It is well worth remembering this during the course and making sure that you get plenty of regular practice at answering listening questions.

Section A: Listening

Just about everyone the world over likes music when they hear it (and most days we hear some music somewhere), but *listening* is something different and sets apart the musical mind. The examiners want to know how precisely you listen to – and understand – the details of music when you hear it played.

In order to do this they will set a range of questions on a variety of musical excerpts. Some questions will offer visual clues in the form of notation – probably a skeleton score which shows the outline of the music, but with some parts omitted – others will require you to rely solely on your aural perception.

This part of the paper is more about skills than knowledge – you won't have to identify the excerpts, for example. However, you will need to know some music theory, such as the different types of cadence. Remember that theory is not much help unless you have trained your ear to recognise the differences in *how such things sound*.

Your teacher will be giving you plenty of practice in class, and practice listening tests are available from the publishers of this book (see *right*) – but there is also much you can do to help yourself. The following table lists some of the various places that you may hear music during your day, and some of the questions you can ask yourself about it:

You can *hear* music while doing other activities and gain pleasure from it, but you are unlikely to notice much musical detail since your brain will be busy on whatever else it is that you are doing.

Listening is a deliberate and intense activity that occurs when you decide to focus on the sound reaching your ears. This cannot be done effectively while looking at something irrelevant, such as a magazine or text message, or while talking.

Remember that half the marks for this paper (amounting to 15% of your AS) are for *listening*, not hearing!

Practice listening tests for this paper will be available from Rhinegold Publishing: www.rhinegold.co.uk

Sources of music	Questions to ask yourself
Radio Television Cinema Mobile phone ring tones Church bells Tones preceding PA announcements Background music in shops and restaurants	Is it major or minor? What is the shape of the melody? What is the texture? Which instruments are being used? What is the metre? What is the character of the rhythmic content? How is the music constructed?

No doubt there will be times when you want (and deserve) just to relax to your favourite music, but now you have chosen to specialise in music by choosing it as an AS option, make sure that on a regular basis you find time to listen to a wide range of music and explore parts of the repertoire that are new to you. This is the equivalent to the background reading you will do for your other subjects. Try some different radio stations, and explore what is available on line. A particularly good resource is the Naxos Music Library (www. naxosmusiclibrary.com): perhaps your school or college subscribes to it. Best of all, try to go to some live music events.

AQA has set out in its specification what aspects of music you should be able to identify aurally. The exercises that follow should help you to pinpoint each of these features before you try questions which combine several of them in a way typical of AS. You could work through these by yourself or with a friend, or your teacher may suggest specific exercises before giving you a sample AS question which incorporates the same musical feature.

> If any of the exercises that follow is a problem for you, turn to the *Music Literacy Workbook* by Rebecca Berkley and Gavin Richards. Rhinegold Publishing, 2007. ISBN 978-1-906178-00-0.

Cadences

Music that is based on one or more major or minor keys is called **tonal**. In tonal music cadences are like punctuation in writing – they help to mark out the sections. A cadence consists of two different chords at the end of a phrase. You need to listen mainly to the progression of chords, as defined by the bass line, since the notes in the tune can vary according to the composer's melodic ideas. You need to be able to recognise the four main types of cadence:

A **perfect cadence** consists of a progression from the dominant chord (V), or dominant seventh (V^7), to the tonic chord (I). It gives a strong sense that the musical phrase has been completed, like a full stop at the end of a sentence.

A **plagal cadence** consists of a progression from the subdominant chord (IV) to the tonic chord (I) and gives an alternative sense of completion to a phrase. The plagal cadence is a little less energetic than the perfect cadence, the note in the melody often being the tonic in both chords.

An **imperfect cadence** consists of a progression that ends on the dominant chord (V). It creates a sense of momentary repose at the end of a phrase, rather like a comma in a sentence. There are various options for the first chord, including I, Ic, ii or IV (Ic is the second inversion of the tonic chord, explained on page 10).

Perfect: V^7 I

Plagal: IV   I

Imperfect: **ii**   **V**   Imperfect: **I**   **V**   Imperfect: **IV**   **V**

An **interrupted cadence** consists of a progression that starts with a dominant chord (V or V^7) that is followed by any chord *except* I – the submediant (vi) is a common choice. It creates a sense of surprise, rather like an exclamation mark, because the ear expects the dominant chord to be followed by a tonic chord.

Interrupted: **V**   **vi**

Exercise 1

Here are two passages featuring a range of cadences. Play them and listen to the cadences. In each passage there is a cadence in every alternate bar. Can you identify them? You may like to work with a friend, each playing a phrase for the other to listen to.

Chord identification

You should be able to identify the primary chords – I, IV and V. In a major key all three will be major triads; in a minor key chords i and iv will be minor, while chord V will usually be major.

> A **triad** is a three-note chord.

If you have a skeleton score which provides the melody you can use this to help work out which chords may fit at each point. Consider the following melody in which you are asked to say which chords occur in the places marked **X**, **Y** and **Z**:

Which primary triads fit these notes? Can you see that only chord IV would fit at **X** and only chord V at **Z**? However, either I or V would fit at **Y**, so here you would need to listen to the recording, checking to see whether chords Y and Z are the same or different. Remember to listen particularly to the bass at this point.

Now have someone play you the version *below*. See if you can confirm aurally that your expectations at **X** and **Z** are correct, and try to decide which of I or V is used at **Y**.

Sometimes the dominant chord will include a 7th (chord V^7). This is something which you need to be able to spot aurally. Try playing the last example again but add an F to chord **Z**. Repeat the passage in both versions and get used to the difference between V and V^7 – it is subtle, but audible. The version without the 7th should sound cleaner, but the 7th gives a greater sense of inevitability to the cadence. What type of cadence is it?

Chord **Y** *above* is a triad of C major (C–E–G) in **root position**, which means that the lowest note, or root, of the chord (C) is also the bass note. If the middle note of the triad (E) had been in the bass, we would have described the chord as being in **first inversion**, and if the top note of the triad (G) had been in the bass we would have described it as being in **second inversion**.

You should also be able to hear the difference between chords in root position and those in first or second inversion. The first inversion is a more gentle version of the chord than the sturdy root position, while the second inversion sounds in need of resolution to another chord.

I(a)   Ib   Ic
root   first   second
position inversion   inversion

Inversions are shown by writing 'b' (first inversion) or 'c' (second inversion) after the chord number. Strictly speaking, root positions should have 'a' after the chord number, but in practice this is usually omitted.

Exercise 2

Identify the following chords and their positions (the first two answers are given). The key is C major. You could either play the chords yourself, as written, or pair up with a friend and listen to each other play the chords in a more random order. Remember it is the bass note which defines what position a chord is in, not the tune.

I   Vb

Now try making up some more chord patterns in other keys using chords I, IV, V and V^7 in root position, first inversion or second inversion, to test your friends with.

A particularly important progression of chords to recognise aurally is Ic–V^7–I which is the boldest of all perfect-cadence ('full stop') patterns. Work out these chords in any major key and play them on the piano. An alternative name for the Ic chord in this progression is a cadential $^6_4$ because the upper notes are a 6th and a 4th above the bass note.

The cadential $^6_4$

Exercise 3

Identify the words on which the following harmonic features occur in the music printed *above*. After you have identified each feature visually, listen to the music being played to you and make sure you can spot each one aurally, too.

➤ The first appearance of chord I in first inversion (chord Ib)

➤ The first appearance of the dominant chord

➤ An interrupted cadence

➤ Two separate cadential $^6_4$ progressions

➤ Two bars of unchanging tonic harmony

➤ Two bars of unchanging dominant 7th harmony

➤ Chord IV preceding a chord of Ic.

Modulations

You need to be able to tell when music has changed key and to recognise whether the new key is the dominant, subdominant or relative minor of the starting key.

Beware of simple descriptions of minor keys as 'sad' – fast music in a minor key may sound angry and exciting, just as slow music in a major key can sound sombre and reflective. You really have to listen carefully to the tonic chord to decide whether the tonality is major or minor.

> Try listening to the *Danse Macabre* by Saint-Saëns or Vivaldi's Violin Concerto in A minor (Op. 3 No. 6) to see how minor keys sound in energetic music.

Distinguishing between modulations to the dominant or the subdominant, both of which will be major if the starting key is major, can seem more challenging.

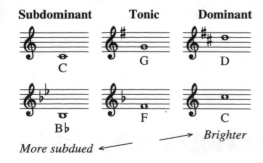

Subdominant   Tonic   Dominant

C   G   D

Bb   F   C

More subdued ←   → *Brighter*

Raising a note by a semitone is done by using either a sharp sign or, if the note is a flat, by using a natural sign.

Lowering a note by a semitone is done by using either a flat sign or, if the note is a sharp, by using a natural sign.

The essential difference is that the dominant key has one more sharp (or one fewer flat) than the tonic and thus sounds brighter. In contrast, the subdominant key has one fewer sharp (or one more flat) than the tonic, and therefore sounds more subdued (see *left*).

You need to train your ear to spot this subtle difference, but there may be some further clues to help. Firstly, if you have a skeleton score, look for any accidentals which may hint at where the music is heading:

➤ The fourth degree of the tonic scale will be raised by a semitone if the music modulates to the dominant

➤ The seventh degree of the tonic scale will be lowered by a semitone if the music modulates to the subdominant

➤ The fifth degree of the tonic scale will be raised by a semitone if the music modulates to the relative minor.

Secondly, consider the structure of the piece. For instance, if it is in binary form and you are approaching the end of the first section (with its double bar) the music is probably modulating to the dominant or (if it started in a minor key) to the relative major.

Exercise 4

Each of the following passages modulates near the end. Listen carefully to them being played and identify the relationship of the new key to the tonic in each case.

You could compose your own short tunes like these, with similar modulations to try out on your friends.

Melodic contour

You need to be able to identify intervals between notes in a melody using the correct technical terms.

You calculate the number of an interval by calling the lower note '1' and counting up the major scale *based on that note* until you reach the higher note. If the upper note occurs in the major scale that began on the lower note, the interval is either major (if it is a 2nd, 3rd, 6th or 7th) or perfect:

> The best way of getting accustomed to melodic intervals is to sing regularly in a choir. This internalises the sound of each interval and, come the silence of the exam room, you can imagine how singing the interval would feel to you.

Unison   Major 2nd *(tone)*   Major 3rd   Perfect 4th   Perfect 5th   Major 6th   Major 7th   Octave

Minor intervals are a semitone lower than their major counterparts:

Minor 2nd *(semitone)*   Minor 3rd   Minor 6th   Minor 7th

If you are sure of the number of the interval, but the upper note is a semitone *higher* than a major or perfect interval, the interval would be called **augmented**. Similarly, if the note is a semitone *lower* than a minor or perfect interval, it is called **diminished**.

Augmented 4th   Diminished 7th

Exercise 5

So much for the theory: what matters is the sound. Here are two melodies with various leaps. Try to identify each bracketed interval in the following melodies:

(a)

(b)

> Being confident at identifying intervals is a huge advantage when it comes to any question that requires you to write down part of the melody in one of the Section A questions.

Melodic decoration

Notes in a melodic line are either

➤ **Harmony notes** – in other words, they are one of the notes of the current chord, or they are

➤ **Non-harmony notes** – these are notes that are not part of the current chord and are therefore dissonant (although the degree of dissonance can be very mild).

You need to be able to spot three types of non-harmony note:

➤ **Passing notes** are dissonances that occur on weak beats and which move *by step* between two harmony notes that are usually a 3rd apart.

In the following phrase, passing notes in bars 1–2 have been marked with an **X**; mark the passing notes in bars 3–4 in the same way:

If a passing note occurs *on* the beat, it is known as an **accented passing note**. It must still move by step between two harmony notes:

➤ **Appoggiaturas** are dissonances that occur on strong beats. They are approached by a leap (upwards or downwards) from the previous note and they then resolve by step to a harmony note.

In the following phrase, the appoggiaturas in bars 1–2 have been marked with an **X**; mark the appoggiaturas in bars 3–4 in the same way:

➤ A **note of anticipation**, as the name suggests, is a forthcoming harmony note that is sounded fractionally early, creating a dissonance with the current chord.

In the following phrase, the anticipations in bars 1–2 have been marked with an **X**; mark those in bars 3–4 in the same way:

Exercise 6

Listen carefully to the following piece being played several times. Mark passing notes in the melody as **P**, appoggiaturas as **App**, and anticipatory notes as **Ant**.

Ornaments

Some types of melodic decoration are indicated by ornament signs. There are three types you should be able to recognise:

➤ A **trill** is a rapid alternation of two adjacent notes, the principal note and the note above.

➤ A **turn** is a graceful pattern of adjacent notes either side of the principal note and is often used towards the end of a long note.

➤ A **mordent** consists of a rapid movement from the principal note to an adjacent note and back.

Make sure you learn these symbols as they may be required for marking up a skeleton score with the ornaments you hear.

Exercise 7

Here is a short tune littered with trills, turns and mordents. Ask someone to play it to you with some of the ornaments omitted. Circle those that are actually played.

Metre

Identifying time signatures should be fairly straightforward at this level. More often than not the first beat of a bar (the downbeat) is given greater stress than any other (not least because this is where the harmony usually changes) and one only has to count the beats between downbeats to work out how many beats there are in a bar.

> Bear in mind that many pieces begin with an anacrusis (upbeat) rather than on the first beat of a bar.

What can cause more difficulty is spotting (and understanding) the difference between simple time and compound time.

➤ In simple time (such as ²₄, ³₄ or ⁴₄) each beat can be divided into two: '1 and 2 and 3 and …'

➤ In compound time (such as ⁶₈) each beat can be divided into three: '1 and a 2 and a …'.

Exercise 8

Both of the pieces on the next page have essentially the same melody, but the first one is in simple time (³₄) whereas the second is in compound time (⁶₈). This puts the accents in different places:

➤ In ³₄ quavers 1, 3 and 5 are accented

➤ In ⁶₈ quavers 1 and 4 are accented.

Listen to these pieces and make sure you can hear the difference in metre. Then ask someone to play just the melodies to you. Can you still tell which one is in simple triple metre (three crotchet beats per bar) and which is in compound duple metre (two dotted crotchet beats per bar)?

Textures

Texture describes the way in which the simultaneous lines of a piece (melody, bass and harmony) relate. The main terms used to identify textures are:

➤ **Monophonic** (an unaccompanied melody)

   ➤ If all the parts in a monophonic texture perform the melody at the same pitch, they are said to be in **unison**

   ➤ If the parts duplicate each other in different registers, they are said to be **doubled in octaves**.

➤ **Homophonic** (one main melody with accompaniment)

   ➤ If the accompaniment follows the same rhythm as the tune (as often heard in hymns) the texture can be described more precisely as **chordal** or **homorhythmic**

   ➤ If the accompaniment has some degree of independence, the texture can be described as **melody-dominated homophony** or **melody and accompaniment**.

➤ **Polyphonic** or **contrapuntal** (several melodic parts heard at the same time)

   ➤ If the parts copy each other a few beats apart, the texture is described as **imitative counterpoint**

   ➤ If totally independent melodies are combined, the texture is described as **free counterpoint**.

When describing contrapuntal music, try to identify the number of simultaneous melodic parts involved – for example, 'two-part counterpoint' or 'four-part counterpoint'.

Textures often change within a piece and are sometimes combined. For instance, even in a basically homophonic passage, a main melody might be accompanied by a **countermelody** to add contrapuntal interest, or might be underpinned by a **pedal**. Or two parts might exchange ideas in **dialogue** above a chordal accompaniment. However, exam questions are likely to focus on clearly identifiable textures rather than on anything complicated!

The following piece uses a variety of textures. Can you identify the texture of each numbered phrase? Try teaming up with other students to play different phrases in turn and agree on what each texture is. You should find that the phrases can be played in different orders which will keep everyone on their toes.

Phrases 5 and 6 have the same texture, but can you say how these two phrases are related?

Instrumentation

Make sure that you are familiar with all the instrumental timbres (tone colours) that you are likely to find in music ranging from pieces for symphony orchestra to songs for jazz ensembles and pop bands. It is necessary to be able to identify not only each instrument, but also some of the different sounds each can make, for example:

➤ **Orchestra**: bowed, pizzicato, muted and tremolo strings, the sounds of different woodwind in very high or low registers, harp arpeggios and harmonics, the continuo instruments (usually harpsichord and cello) in Baroque music, and so on

➤ **Jazz ensemble**: glissando, muted brass, sticks or brushes on the drums, and so on

➤ **Pop music**: guitar effects, synthesised sounds, the different timbres in a drum kit, and so on.

Compositional devices

You could also be asked to identify compositional devices of the type that should be familiar from your GCSE studies, such as sequence, ostinato (or riff), canon, syncopation and pedal.

Answering the questions

Each extract of music will be played several times, perhaps up to four or five, with pauses between each repetition. Use the pauses to check that you understand the various questions and to decide what to focus on during the next playing. It should be possible to listen out for several specific features in each playing.

At some point there will be a question asking you to fill in some missing notes on a skeleton score. This is often worth several marks and can be quite challenging. Keep calm, and consider each of the following angles:

➢ What is the overall shape of the melody at the place in question: rising, falling, a scale, an arpeggio?

➢ Is the first of the missing notes higher, lower, or the same as the printed note immediately before the gap?

➢ Is the last of the missing notes higher, lower, or the same as the printed note immediately after the gap?

➢ Do the notes you have written fit harmonically with any given notes in the accompaniment at this point?

Once you have heard an excerpt for the last time it is important to clear your mind and move on to the next set of questions. Read the text and any given notation carefully and be ready to make constructive use of the first playing of the new extract.

For definitions of technical terms in music, together with notated and recorded examples so that you can both read and hear them, see the *Dictionary of Music in Sound* by David Bowman. Rhinegold Publishing. ISBN 978-0-946890-87-3.

Section B: Area of Study 1

Introduction

Area of Study 1 is a compulsory set work. For examinations in June 2009, 2010 and 2011 this will be the first and third movements of Mozart's Symphony No. 41 in C, K551, nicknamed the *Jupiter* Symphony. It is expected that a different work will be set for exams in June 2012 and after.

There will be two questions on this work in Section B, each worth 20 marks, from which you have to answer **one** (you will be allowed to refer to an *unmarked* score). The questions are likely to ask you to discuss Mozart's approach to one of the main elements of composition: melody, harmony and tonality, rhythm and metre, texture, instrumentation and timbre, and form. It is also advisable to know something of the historical context of the piece. It is probable that one question will be on the first movement, and the other on the third movement, but don't rule out the chances of a more general question for which you could draw on both movements.

> K551 refers to the number given to this symphony in a catalogue of Mozart's compositions compiled by an Austrian music scholar named Köchel.

The composer

Wolfgang Amadeus Mozart (1756–1791) is one of the most famous composers of the Classical period, which extended from the middle of the 18th century until about 1820. The Classical style in music is characterised by clear, melody-dominated structures.

Mozart was born in Salzburg, Austria. The son of a professional violinist, he showed an early talent for music, and by the age of five could compose and perform simple keyboard pieces. While still a child, Mozart travelled around Europe giving concerts arranged by his father. In 1764–1765 the Mozarts stayed in London, where Wolfgang wrote his first symphony at the age of eight.

In 1773, at the age of 17, Mozart became a musician at the court of the Prince-Archbishop of Salzburg. The position involved writing church music, but Mozart also composed numerous orchestral and chamber works, and several operas – a genre in which he was to write some of his greatest music.

Mozart was not well paid and he found life in Salzburg restrictive and provincial. In 1781 he moved to the Austrian capital, Vienna, to establish a career as a freelance musician. There he met Haydn, one of the most respected composers of the day. Although Haydn was 24 years older than Mozart, the two became friends and each learned much from the other.

Mozart was initially very successful in Vienna, particularly when he appeared as the soloist in his own concertos for piano and orchestra. However, public taste was fickle and he began to find it increasingly difficult to make a living. When fever struck late in 1791 the medicine of the day could do little for him, and he died on 5 December. Although only 35 when he died, Mozart left more than 600 works, covering every significant musical genre of the day: operas, church music, symphonies, concertos, quartets, quintets and sonatas.

> For a highly enjoyable insight into Mozart's life, find time to watch the 1984 film *Amadeus* based on the play by Peter Shaffer: it won eight Oscars. It forms a great introduction to much of Mozart's music, but take some of the storyline with a pinch of salt!
>
> Remember that exam questions will focus on specific technical aspects of the *Jupiter* Symphony – there is no need to memorise details of Mozart's biography or to learn the names and dates of his other works.

The symphony

The symphony has, throughout most of its 250-year history, been regarded as one of the most important genres of orchestral music. Haydn, who wrote at least 104 symphonies, revealed the potential of the genre, while Mozart composed at least 41 symphonies. They were followed by Beethoven, whose nine symphonies include some of the most famous of all works in the genre. During the 19th century, and on into the 20th century, the symphony became regarded as the type of work in which any serious orchestral composer was expected to excel.

By the late 18th century, most symphonies were written in the format seen in your set work: four separate substantial sections, known as **movements**, played with a short silence between them. The movements are contrasted in mood but are linked by being in the same, or related, keys – there was not normally any melodic link between the movements at this time. A typical symphony of the Classical period can take between 15 and 30 minutes to perform.

The character of the four movements usually followed a standard pattern in the late 18th century:

➢ 1st movement: a weighty allegro, sometimes preceded by a slow introduction

➢ 2nd movement: a slow movement, perhaps marked adagio or andante, and sometimes in theme-and-variations form

➢ 3rd movement: a lively dance form, based on the minuet

➢ 4th movement: a very fast, light finale, perhaps marked molto allegro or presto.

The orchestra in the Classical period

The rise of the symphony coincides with a significant development in the history of the orchestra.

In the early 18th century, the Baroque orchestra usually consisted of a small group of strings supported by a harpsichord, with the occasional addition of a few wind instruments (most likely oboes).

The late 18th century orchestra was larger, with many more wind instruments, and as a consequence the harmonic infill supplied by a harpsichord or other keyboard instrument became unnecessary.

The increase in size came about partly through the patronage of music by wealthy aristocrats who employed their own bands of musicians – the larger the group, the greater the prestige. But other reasons included the increasing popularity of public concerts in venues that required a larger orchestra, a taste for a wider range of orchestral tone colour and improvements to the mechanisms of wind instruments that increased their reliability and versatility.

As part of this expansion the wind section was now a permanent fixture of the orchestra. This would regularly include two oboes, two bassoons and two horns, and as such was capable of providing a good full orchestral sound in conjunction with the strings, or a contrast to the strings when used alternately. Flutes also appeared with increasing frequency, but the clarinet was still rather new and rather rare in the Classical orchestra.

Trumpets and timpani might also appear. They are particularly likely for music in D major or C major and, sure enough, Mozart makes use of them in the *Jupiter*.

Brass instruments did not have valves at this time, so horns and trumpets were restricted to the pitches that occur naturally in the harmonic series, of which Mozart uses the notes shown *right*. Notice that he used F(♮) rather than F♯ for the note marked ∗ – this requires the player to adjust the position of the hand in the bell of the instrument in order to lower the F♯ by a semitone.

This limited set of pitches is the main reason why the brass in this work, as in most others of the period:

➤ Seldom play melodic material and

➤ Are silent if the music moves far from the tonic key.

Mozart used clarinets in a number of his works, but not in the *Jupiter*. Clarinettists may like to listen to Mozart's Symphony No. 39, in which he used them in place of oboes.

The *Jupiter* Symphony

The *Jupiter* was Mozart's last symphony. In 1788, while at the height of his powers, he wrote three major symphonies in just over six weeks during the summer – No. 39 in E♭, No. 40 in G minor and No. 41 in C, known as the *Jupiter*. None of these works was commissioned and it is not known why Mozart wrote them – it is possible he intended to include them in concerts he was planning in Vienna, but it is unclear if these actually took place and so we do not know whether Mozart ever heard the *Jupiter* performed.

The work's nickname is also a mystery. It was almost certainly not invented by Mozart and seems to have appeared in the early 19th century. Jupiter, or Jove, was the supreme god of Roman mythology, lord of heaven and bringer of light. The sparkling energy, first heard in the opening of the symphony, but more sustained in the work's finale, perhaps suggested this name for the piece.

Although you only have to study the first and third movements, you should listen to the whole symphony from time to time. The slow movement is full of charm and elegance, while the symphony is most famed for its extraordinary finale.

One of the best ways of getting to know a work is to perform it. The first movement requires technically advanced players, but the third movement could be rescored for a variety of small groups and this would also provide a useful exercise in arranging.

In order to gain a historical perspective on this work, you may like to listen to these other symphonies from the Classical period, all of which are in the same key as the *Jupiter*:

Haydn: Symphony No. 69 in C *Laudon* (1779)

Mozart: Symphony No. 36 in C *Linz* (1783)

Beethoven: Symphony No.1 in C (1799–1800).

Scores and recordings

You can study Mozart's *Jupiter* Symphony from any edition, and a wide choice of recordings is available. If possible, try to compare several different performances – especially one played on period instruments with one played on modern instruments. If you don't already have a score and CD, the Eulenburg Audio+Score edition (EAS 1), published in 2006, offers a clear, authoritative score packaged with a good recording on the Naxos label for a very modest price.

There are a large number of books available on Mozart's music. The following are particularly useful for additional reading on the *Jupiter* Symphony:

Mozart's Symphonies: Context, Performance, Practice, Reception by Neal Zaslaw. Oxford: Clarendon Press, 1989. ISBN 0-19-816286-3 617.

Mozart: The 'Jupiter' Symphony by Elaine Sisman. Cambridge Music Handbooks, Cambridge University Press, 1993. ISBN 0-521-40924-1.

The orchestra required for a performance of the *Jupiter* Symphony is:

> 1 flute
> 2 oboes
> 2 bassoons
> 2 horns
> 2 trumpets
> timpani
> strings

The size of the string section is not usually specified in orchestral music, but for a work of this period there typically might have been about 22 string players: 12 violins (divided into six first violins and six second violins), four violas, four cellos and two double basses. Modern symphony orchestras generally have at least twice this number of string players.

Instrument names in scores are usually printed in Italian. Most are so close to their English equivalents that their meanings are obvious, but note the following exceptions:

Fagotto is a bassoon
Corno is a horn (*not* a cornet)
Tromba is a trumpet (*not* a trombone)
Contrabasso is a double bass.

Following the score

Orchestral scores are laid out on sets of staves called systems. Most editions of the *Jupiter* Symphony use ten staves in a system when the whole orchestra is playing, and include two such systems on each page. Staves are sometimes omitted when instruments are resting and this may allow an extra system to fit on the page – watch out for this when following the score.

When reading the score while listening to the music, concentrate on the first-violin part, letting your eye take in the other staves when the focus of interest moves to a different part. You may find it helpful to mark the start of each first-violin stave (or other important part) with a highlighter pen if you find the score difficult to follow.

All of the instruments sound at their printed pitch except horns and double basses, both of which sound an octave lower than written.

Watch out for the alto clef in the viola part – it indicates that the middle line of the stave is middle C. Look at bars 1–2 of the first movement: the violas are playing exactly the same notes as the violins. What note do the violas play in bars 3–4?

In much of the work, cellos and double basses play the same notes, although the basses sound an octave lower. Passages marked 'Vc.' are for cellos only and the word tutti (meaning 'all') indicates the point where the double basses join in once again. However, the double basses occasionally have an independent part (as in bars 39–46 of the first movement), often when the cellos are in their high, tenor register. This was one of the new orchestral effects that composers were starting to explore in the larger orchestras of the late 18th century.

Here are some other details in the score about which you should be aware (bar numbers of examples refer to the first movement):

a2	oboes bar 2	The two wind players are to play the same notes
♪	violins bars 17–18	Each crotchet is to be played as four repeated semiquavers
1	oboes bar 24	A passage to be played by just the first of the two wind players
tr	timpani bars 83–84	A trill sign for timpani indicates a drum roll on a single pitch
pizz.	basses bar 101	An abbreviation for pizzicato (pluck the strings)
arco	cellos bar 101	Bow the strings (rather than plucking them)

In addition, notice that string players sometimes have to play two notes at the same time, known as **double-stopping** (violins, bar 5) or even three notes at the same time, known as **triple-stopping** (first violins, bar 9).

Answer the following questions on the background to Mozart's *Jupiter* Symphony.

1. Which composer from the Classical period greatly influenced Mozart?

2. What is the standard format of a late 18th century symphony?

3. List the instruments required for a performance of the *Jupiter* Symphony.

4. Why was it that the trumpets and horns in Mozart's day could play only certain notes?

5. Why is Mozart's 41st Symphony called the *Jupiter*?

6. Explain precisely what (a) the violins and (b) the lower strings are required to play in bars 273–274 of the *first movement* of the *Jupiter* Symphony.

First movement

Structure

There is no slow introduction – Mozart starts the symphony by launching straight into the opening movement, which is marked allegro vivace (fast and lively).

This movement is in **sonata form** – the most common structure used in the Classical period for the first movement of sonatas, symphonies and other multi-movement works.

Sonata form evolved in the mid 18th century as a way to structure relatively long movements on the basis of key. There are three main sections:

Exposition – in the first part of which the tonic key is established and the main theme introduced. Midway through this section the music modulates to a related key (usually the dominant if the tonic key is major) and often, but not always, a contrasting theme is introduced. The section ends in this new key, giving the sense that the music has moved away from its starting point. In works of the Classical period, the exposition is usually repeated before continuing with the …

Development – in which thematic material from the exposition is transformed in various ways and more distant keys are intrduced, giving the sense that the music has journeyed further away from home.

Recapitulation – in which most of the material from the exposition returns, but now modified in order to stay centred on the tonic key throughout. This gives the sense that the musical journey has ended by returning home. The tonic key may be reinforced still further in a concluding section called the **coda**.

This simple plan of conflicting and resolving keys is sometimes called the 'sonata principle' – it is not a rigid form, and it proved to be flexible enough to accommodate many different types and styles of music throughout the Classical and Romantic periods, and even on into the early 20th century.

Before we look at the movement in detail, it would be a good idea to mark the starts of these three main sections into your score:

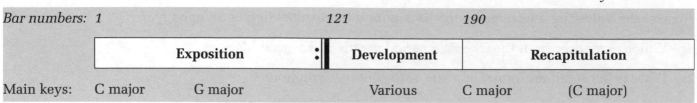

Bar numbers:	1			121		190	
	Exposition		:‖	Development		Recapitulation	
Main keys:	C major	G major		Various	C major	(C major)	

Listen to the whole movement while following the score. Can you tell that each section fulfils a discrete function – a beginning, middle and end?

Exposition

The exposition begins with the **first subject** – a group of thematic ideas in the tonic key. We can divide it into two sections: bars 1–8 and bars 9–23.

First subject   Bars 1–8   A call to attention from the full orchestra in bars 1–2 loudly announces the tonic. It is answered by quiet strings in bars 3–4, who end on dominant harmony. These four bars are then repeated, but this time starting on the dominant (bar 5) and ending on the tonic (bar 8).

The first four bars are like a question – they sound incomplete because they end on dominant harmony. And the next four bars are like an answer, because they end on tonic harmony.

Technically, the question phrase is called an **antecedent** and the answer phrase is known as a **consequent**. This pairing of balanced phrases is called **periodic phrasing** and can be found throughout the works of Mozart and his contemporaries – it is one of the most characteristic features of the Classical style.

The underlying harmonies of bars 1–8 could not define the tonic key more clearly:

Brass and timpani hammer out the tonic three times at the start, while the rest of the orchestra reinforce the key of C major by rising from dominant to tonic in triplet semiquavers, shown in example *(a) left*.

The effect is rather rustic: as though a concert was about to be given by the village band. But the answering phrase (bars 3–4) is altogether more sophisticated and charming. Only violins, violas and cellos play, the dynamic is $\boldsymbol{p}$, and the melody is decorated with expressive dissonances: in example *(b) left* the note marked **1** is a suspension and the note marked **2** is an appoggiatura.

As we shall see, Mozart later makes extensive use of both of these contrasting ideas.

As previously noted, bars 5–8 are a restatement of the first four bars, adapted to fit with a dominant-to-tonic progression. Note that the passing F♯s in bar 5 are purely chromatic – they reinforce the role of G as the dominant, but there is no modulation to G major yet.

The second half of the first subject (bars 9–23) is a full-blooded tutti fanfare that seems to be in celebratory mood.

Bars 9–23   First subject

Bars 9–14 outline a simple pattern of primary triads (I–IV–V–I–IV–V) over an articulated **tonic pedal** (that is, sounded as a rhythm rather than as a continuous note). Above this is heard:

➢ A confident dotted pattern for wind and timpani (note how the trumpets and timpani only join in on beats 2 and 3)

➢ Extrovert double- and triple-stopped chords for first violins on beats 1 and 4 (when trumpets and timpani are not playing)

➢ Scurrying downward demisemiquavers for second violins and violas (mirroring the rising triplet semiquavers of bar 1).

Bars 15–23 hammer home the fact that this symphony is going to be in C major by using only tonic and dominant harmony. Mozart winds up the tension by increasing the **harmonic rhythm** (the rate at which chords change) before ending on chord V in bars 22–23:

9	10	11	12	13	14	15	16	17	18	19	20	21	22	23
I	IV	V	I	IV	V	I V	I V	I	I	V I	V I	V I V I V I V I	V	V

Notice the change in texture from bar 17^2–19^1, where the arpeggio-like figure is played in bare octaves (except for the timpani, which has only the notes G and C available) with energetic semiquavers in the violins. Notice also the syncopation in bars 19–20 caused by the off-beat wind chords, which adds further excitement to this cadential passage. The pause on an unharmonised dominant in bar 23 prepares for the return of the tonic key at the start of the next section.

Superscript numbers refer to beats in the bar, so 17^2 means bar 17, beat 2.

Bars 24–55 form a lengthy **transition** to the dominant, the key in which the exposition will eventually end. It begins with a varied reprise of the opening bars, in which the former contrast between motifs *(a)* and *(b)* is much diluted: the dynamic is now consistently *p* and the melody is played only by violins (alternately in unison and in octaves). Meanwhile a **countermelody**, played by flute and first oboe in 6ths and 3rds, floats above the main melody. Its phrases bridge the silence between motifs *(a)* and *(b)*, reducing their contrast still further. In bar 31 it seamlessly merges into an accompaniment figure of three repeated crotchets that Mozart will reuse later.

Bars 24–55   Transition

The texture in these bars is very delicate. The two melodic lines provide a simple counterpoint, lightly supported by a tonic arpeggio on horns in bar 24 and a dominant arpeggio on bassoons in bar 28. The vast majority of the music is in the treble register.

If you refer to motifs by letters such as 'a' and 'b' in an exam answer, you ***must*** state exactly which notes you mean – for example, 'Motif a (the first violin melody in bars 1–2¹) …'. If you don't do this, the examiner will have no idea what you are referring to, and you would therefore risk losing marks.

In bars 30–31 Mozart subtly changes the intervals of the original melody, while still preserving its general contour. This is the trigger for four bars of chromatic harmony (bars 31–34) in which Mozart detaches the second half of motif *(b)* and repeats it in **sequence**.

This process of detaching part of a previous idea to use in its own right is a compositional technique known as **fragmentation**.

The harmony of bars 31–35^2 is based on a **circle-of-5ths** progression which is disguised by:

➢ Appoggiaturas at the start of every bar in the melody

➢ A bass part (for bassoon) which descends chromatically instead of outlining the roots of the chords.

Mozart's harmonic thinking is easier to understand if we add those roots and respace the inner parts – in the following example, the basic chords are shown with grey shading:

The wind drop out in bars 35–36, ready to make a fresh impact at the start of the next phrase, which is a loud tutti.

In bars 37–38 motif *(a)* appears again in combination with the countermelody, but now based on the dominant. This leads straight into a development of motif *(b)* in rising sequence. After three repetitions (bars 38^4–40^3, 40^4–42^3 and 42^4–44^3), Mozart detaches the last three notes of *(a)* to use in descending sequence (bars 44^4–45^3 and 45^4–46^3) – another example of fragmentation.

The whole of this melody is played by a forceful team of second violins (in their rich bottom octave), cellos (liberated from the bass part and playing in their warm tenor register) and bassoons (providing a reedy cutting edge). It is doubled an octave and a 6th higher by first violins, and accompanied by a pedal on G duplicated across five octaves (see *left* – note that horns in C and doubles basses both sound an octave lower than written).

The third and final section of the transition (bars 49–55) is adapted from the fanfare-like passage at the end of the first subject (starting at bar 9). Here, though, the key is G major and the chords are V and Ic in that key, and the pedal on D. These seven bars function as a passage of **dominant preparation**, creating a sense of expectation that the dominant key is about to appear – which, indeed, it does with the arrival of the second subject in bar 56.

There are two final points to note about the transition:

➢ Although the development is still some way off, it is clear that Mozart is already starting to develop ideas from his first subject during the transition – a technique that became increasingly common in sonata-form movements of the later Classical period

➢ After the transition ends in bar 55 on chord V of G major (creating an imperfect cadence) there are three beats of total silence to mark the end of this section.

Bars 56–100   Second subject

The G major second subject is lightly scored and marked $\boldsymbol{p}$. Bars 56–57 are in a thin, two-part texture and when the lower strings enter in bar 58 they **imitate** the first violin's ascending chromatic figure.

The first phrase ends with an imperfect cadence in bars 60^3–61 and is, unusually, six bars long. A chromatic link in bar 61 leads to a varied repeat of the first phrase, in which the first-violin melody is doubled by the first bassoon at a lower octave. This time the last bar of the phrase (bar 67) is modified to end on chord V^7d of G major, which triggers a four-bar extension before the expected perfect cadence (Ic–V^7–I) is reached in bars $70–71^1$. The first-violin melody in these four bars is doubled by the flute an octave higher as well as by the bassoon an octave lower, creating a delightful timbre that is typical of Mozart's orchestration.

> The bassoon is initially two octaves below the first violin, in order to avoid high notes unavailable on most bassoons of the day. It changes to one octave below in bar 64.

> Chord V^7d means the third inversion of the dominant seventh.

Notice that the result of answering a six-bar phrase with a ten-bar phrase is a 16-bar section – the same as the length that would have resulted from using four four-bar phrases.

Lower strings in bar 71 provide a link (reminiscent of motif *(b)* from the first subject) to the four-bar violin melody in bars 72–75. This cadential phrase features three crotchets on the same pitch, an idea heard earlier in bar 67, and earlier still in the accompaniment to bars 31–34. When this phrase is repeated in bars 76–79, the ending is changed to veer away from the expected G major cadence to end with three repeated crotchet chords on V^7d of C major.

This would be entirely the wrong place to return to the tonic, as Mozart knew very well, but he teases his audience with an abrupt and total silence in bar 80 (an effect known as a **general pause**) followed by the *minor* version of chord I (C minor, bar 81) in a loud and dramatic tutti.

Bars 81–100 provide a striking contrast to the delicate first part of the second subject. The music remains on a chord of C minor for two bars, the first significant use of a minor triad in the piece. It is as though a thunderstorm has suddenly erupted. But the harmony then moves chromatically to a chord of C major (bars 85–86), which turns out to be chord IV of G major, at the start of the weightiest perfect cadence we have heard yet – it is as though the sun has broken through the thunderclouds. Here is a harmonic outline of this passage:

> Listen to role of the timpani in this passage: it underlines the dark minor chord with a dotted rhythm in bar 81, adds to the climax with a long roll in bars 83–84, and then confidently marks out each beat of the majestic bars 85–86. It doesn't play in bars 87–88 since, in Mozart's day, only two pitches (tonic and dominant of a movement's main key) were normally available. However, it is ready to underpin the tonic of the second subject (G) once the cadence resolves.

The third section of the second subject, begining in bar 89, is a more excited version of the passage from bar 39 of the transition: it has a similar texture of a melody doubled in compound 6ths and a tonic pedal heard in several octaves.

Bar 3:

Bar 90:

diminution sequence

Fragmentation is used again here. In bar 90 Mozart detaches the first half of the dotted motif first heard in bar 3 and then repeats it in **rhythmic diminution** (notes of half the length). The diminution is then repeated in rising sequence (see *left*).

This entire bar is then repeated in rising sequence in bars 91 and 92, creating a sense of great urgency. A cadential figure in bars 92–93 completes this five-bar phrase, the cadence of which overlaps with the beginning of a varied repeat of the phrase in bar 94. This starts with the same melodic sequence, but is rescored so that the melody (now in 3rds) is taken by the lower strings and woodwind, thereby freeing up the first violins to re-energise the tonic pedal by reiterating it in **syncopation**.

Just when we are expecting a culminating cadence the tutti breaks off, leaving the first violins to play an unaccompanied descending arpeggiation of chord V^7, which leads to another general pause.

Closing theme   Bars 101–111

This leads the way to a new idea, often called a **closing theme**, which starts in bar 101, still in the second-subject key of G major. Mozart took the tune from a comic song he had written earlier for inclusion in someone else's opera. Here it seems almost like an after-thought, coming so late in the exposition – but, as we shall see, it will become much more significant later.

The typical periodic phrasing of the Classical period may not be immediately obvious in this theme because each of its phrases starts with a long anacrusis. However, since there are eight beats (two bars' worth of notes) in each phrase, as shown *below*, we still describe these as two-bar phrases. There are four two-bar phrases, the first three of which are almost identical:

The melody is played by the violins in octaves over a simple tonic-and-dominant harmonisation. Cellos provide a legato broken-chord accompaniment while pizzicato violas and double basses pick-out the root of the chord at the start of each bar. The oboes sustain an **inverted pedal** on the dominant (D) once the tune has got going and the first bassoon joins in at bar 105, doubling the melody at a lower octave. This is another passage that illustrates Mozart's skill in delicate orchestration. Notice also how his choice of slurred and staccato articulation brings out the charm of this theme.

The last two bars of this new tune are repeated (with the flute joining in to brighten the timbre) before the full orchestra returns for the final time in bar 111.

Codetta   Bars 111–120

A **codetta** is a short coda (concluding section) which here marks the end of the exposition by reinforcing the dominant key with a series of cadential figures. The one-bar motif in bars 111^2–112^1 is decorated with chromatic notes and harmonised in 3rds, and it is then treated as a descending sequence in the next bar. A dominant pedal spans both of these bars and leads to a short cadential figure in bars 113^2–114^1.

These three bars are repeated exactly, and this time the last chord of the cadence (on the first beat of bar 117) overlaps with the start of the final phrase of the exposition. This is derived from bars 15–16 at the end of the first subject, although the key is now G major and the scurrying demisemiquavers are given more sparkle by being assigned to the first violins in a relatively high register. The whole exposition is then repeated.

Exercise 11

1. Explain the terms antecedent, consequent and periodic phrasing, giving examples of each from the first subject of this work.

2. Which instrument plays the *lowest* notes in bars 24–25?

3. Why is it easy not to notice that the transition has begun?

4. On the first beat of bar 35, the violins play a G against the notes A and C in the lower strings. What name is given to this type of melodic decoration?

5. How should the double basses play the G pedal in bars 39–46?

6. How does the chord in bar 81 relate to the key of the symphony?

7. Which section is harmonically more complex: the first subject or the transition?

8. What accounts for the second subject being so much longer than the first subject?

9. What technique do the second violins have to use in the codetta?

10. What is the purpose of the several short silences in the exposition?

Development

The development is the part of sonata form in which themes are transformed and various more distant keys are introduced. The latter becomes obvious as four notes for woodwind in octaves link the exposition, which ended in G major, to the first section of the development, much of which is in the remote key of E♭ major.

Bars 121–160

However, at first Mozart is unconcerned with developing themes. This surprising change of key is enough to show that the musical journey is continuing, and so bars 123–132 simply consist of a restatement of the closing theme from the exposition, transposed to E♭ major, and with a few small changes in instrumentation.

The first *thematic* development begins in bar 133, when the gentle mood of the previous section is interrupted with a lively **dialogue** between upper and lower strings, based on bar 108 from the closing theme of the exposition.

Dialogue is a texture in which motifs are passed between different parts.

Mozart develops this simple idea over the next 28 bars in one of the harmonically most complicated sections of the movement. As you read the next few paragraphs, refer to the skeleton score below. The bottom stave of each system outlines the underlying harmony – you could try playing this stave along with the recording (or ask friends to play the two upper parts with you) as this will help you to understand the harmonic progressions in this passage.

The importance of this passage is not its complexity but the way that Mozart transforms the simple cadential figure from bar 108 – almost too innocuous to be noticed at the time – into one of the most energetic sections of the entire movement. However, we need to understand how he does this.

In bars 133–138, the motif from bar 108 is exchanged between violins and lower strings in dialogue. Mozart winds up the tension by using a rising sequence that ascends from E♭ major, through F minor to G minor throughout these six bars.

In bar 139, Mozart detaches the first half of the motif and adapts it to form a falling two-beat melodic sequence that is imitated by lower strings. The whole of bars 139–140 are then repeated in sequence (melodic and harmonic) a tone lower in bars 141–142.

Starting from bar 139 Mozart also underpins the counterpoint with a **circle-of-5ths** progression, initially with one chord per bar, but then becoming more urgent with two changes of harmony per bar in bars 143–144.

> In a circle of 5ths, roots of successive chords can either fall in 5ths or rise in 4ths. For example, when a chord of G is followed by a chord of C, the root can either fall a 5th from G to C or rise a 4th from G to the C above.

Having reached C minor (the relative minor of E♭ major) at the perfect cadence in bars 144^3–145, the music rapidly modulates upwards in perfect 5ths (C minor – G minor – D minor – A minor) as the counterpoint continues. Notice the inclusion of bar 107 from the closing theme in the bass part of bar 147, echoed in modified form by the violins two bars later.

Despite the energy and excitement of this passage, the brass and timpani are silent. This is because the limited pitches they had available at this time include few useful notes to contribute while the development is visiting keys so remote from the tonic.

The woodwind largely make up for this with a chordal accompaniment to the counterpoint that has a character of its own:

➢ From bar 133, they articulate the harmonies in a dotted rhythm reminiscent of the pattern they played in bars 9–14; like the string parts, this is treated in dialogue, alternating between one bar of treble pitch (flute and oboes) and one of lower pitch (bassoons combined with oboes in a lower register)

➢ From bar 139, the woodwind have long sustained harmony notes which are the perfect foil to the active string parts which go into overdrive at this point

➢ From bar 147, on-beat woodwind chords alternate firstly with off-beat violin chords (double- and triple-stopped) and then with off-beat bass notes.

The imperfect cadence in A minor (bars 152^4–153^1) is repeated in decorated form over a dominant pedal by first the upper strings and then the woodwind, as the texture thins. After this, as the quaver pattern of the previous section continues, Mozart moves chromatically from chord V of A minor (bar 157) to V^7 of F major (bar 160) ready for what the unwary might think is the recapitulation – except that it is *p* and in the wrong key (F major). Mozart is teasing his audience again!

> The first chord of this cadence, on the last beat of bar 152, is a chromatic chord known as an **augmented 6th**. Here it consists of F–A–D♯, the outer notes of which form the interval of an augmented 6th. There are several types of augmented 6th chord; this three-note version is known as an 'Italian 6th'.

Bars 161–181   The version of the first subject heard in bars 161–166 is actually a transposition of the start of the transition (from bar 24), with the countermelody reallocated to the bassoons. Any lingering doubt that this might be the recapitulation is swept aside when Mozart starts to develop bars 165–166 in rising sequence (bars 167–168 and 169–170). As in bars 133–139 in the first part of the development, this rising sequence increases the intensity, as does the first bassoon part which rises chromatically throughout bars 165–170.

Chord V^7 of A minor in bar 170 resolves to chord I in the next bar and, still paralleling that earlier passage in development, Mozart again releases the tension by using a circle-of-5ths progression (B–E–A–D–G–C), which this time includes passing chromaticism between some of the main chords.

The melody played by the violins unites the rising triplet figure from bar 1 with the falling demisemiquaver figure from the inner string parts of bar 9, and falls in a succession of two-bar sequences over the circle-of-5ths harmony. Another skeleton score will help to make all of this clear:

Although this passage does not have the contrapuntal texture of the earlier development section, it bristles with energy, partly due to the rapidly-moving melody, but more because of the woodwind's off-beat chords: they only play on the beat in alternate bars. When they do so, Mozart resourcefully finds available notes on the horns and trumpets that fit the harmony to give these chords extra bite.

From bar 177, the brass chords become more frequent and the timpani join in. Another augmented 6th chord appears in bar 178 (A♭–C–E♭–F♯) – this four-note version is known as a 'German 6th' and the two notes that form the augmented 6th, A♭ and F♯, move outwards by a semitone to G (bar 179) as Mozart begins a passage of dominant preparation for the eventual return of C major.

Ascending and descending versions of the demisemiquaver figure appear in the bass (bars 179–180), followed by a new variant of the bar 108 motif for the first violins – both being accompanied V[7]–I progressions in G major.

A six-bar dominant pedal for horns, later supported by trumpets and timpani, starts in bar 183. Above this the woodwind continue to develop the quaver pattern that has featured in so much of the development. Finally, descending scales of C major in bar 188 lead back to the tonic for the start of the recapitulation.

Before continuing, let's summarise our findings about the development. The last column in the following table refers to the mood of each of its five sections. Notice how carefully Mozart controls the emotional ebb and flow of the music, sandwiching two sections of intensive development – (b) and (d) – between more relaxed linking passages:

> Mozart achieves an elegant symmetry between his two main development passages (bars 133–153[1] and 161–181[1]).
>
> The first is 21 bars long. It starts in E♭ major with a three-fold rising sequence based on a two-bar motif and continues over an extended circle of 5ths. It ends with an augmented 6th chord that resolves to chord V of A minor.
>
> The second is 21 bars long. It starts in F major and, after a few bars, includes a three-fold rising sequence based on a two-bar motif and continues over an extended circle of 5ths. Shortly before the end, an augmented 6th chord resolves to a chord of G major (which later becomes chord V of C major).

(a)	Bars 123–133[1]	A restatement of the closing theme of the exposition (bar 101) transposed to E♭ major	Gentle
(b)	Bars 133–153[1]	Development of bar 108 from the closing theme of the exposition, using dialogue and counterpoint, and modulating widely	Stormy
(c)	Bars 153–160	Modulating link, still based on the motif from bar 108	Gentle
(d)	Bars 161–181[1]	Development of first subject, starting in F major and modulating widely before ending in G major	Starts gently but becomes stormy
(e)	Bars 181–188	Dominant preparation for the recapitulation, based on the motif from bar 108	Gentle

Exercise 12

1. Which main theme from the exposition is *not* explored in the development?

2. Name the two main keys used in the development section.

3. Explain the term dialogue and give an example of its use in the development.

4. Look at the circle of 5ths in the music example on page 30. If Mozart had consistently used falling perfect 5ths and rising perfect 4ths, what should the first note on the lowest stave of bar 144 have been? Why do you think Mozart used D at this point in the circle of 5ths?

5. Explain why bars 183–188 can be described as 'dominant preparation'.

6. How does Mozart bring a sense of symmetry and balance to the development section?

The recapitulation

It is clear the recapitulation begins in bar 189 because the first subject returns *f* and in the tonic key. The recapitulation is essentially a repeat of the exposition but modified so that it ends in the tonic key rather than the dominant:

Section	Exposition	Recapitulation	Comments on the recapitulation
First subject	Bars 1–23	Bars 189–211	Identical to exposition
Transition	Bars 24–55	Bars 212–243	Same length as exposition, but modified to start in C minor, end in C major and avoid modulating to V
Second subject	Bars 56–100	Bars 244–288	Same length as exposition, but a 5th lower (centred on C rather than G) and with changes in scoring
Closing theme	Bars 101–111	Bars 289–299	Same length as exposition, but a 5th lower (in the tonic key of C major) and with changes in scoring
Codetta / Coda	Bars 111–120	Bars 299–313	Similar to the codetta, but transposed to C major and expanded into a coda that emphasises the tonic key

Some of the rescoring in the recapitulation results from the need to avoid parts going too low due to the change of key, but Mozart also uses the opportunity to vary instrumental doublings. Another factor is that the brass and timpani have more notes available when the music is in C, rather than G major, and can therefore be more involved towards the end of the movement.

Transition   Bars 212–243 The normal expectation in a sonata-form recapitulation is that the second part of the transition will be modified in order to introduce the second subject in the tonic instead of in the dominant.

However, Mozart again seems intent on using development in all sections of the movement, since he plunges straight into C minor at bar 212, opening up a whole new tonal world of flat keys. The sense of something new here is reinforced by some exquisite counterpoint, consisting of an interlocking chain of suspensions for violins over another circle-of-5ths progression:

Using the dominant (bar 211) to introduce a sudden change of mode from major to minor (bar 212) was one of the distinctive new features in music of the Classical period.

Despite this diversion, at bar 225 the music is back to where it would have been had Mozart simply copied out the first part of the original transition – in fact, all of bars 225–233 are identical to bars 37–45. The significant tonal change occurs in bars 234^4–236^1, after which Mozart is able to adapt the final bars of the transition to end with a series of Ic–V chords over a dominant pedal in C major, rather than in G major.

Compare bars 234^4–243 with bars 46^4–55 and notice how Mozart moves the demisemiquaver figure into a much higher and more prominent register in the recapitulation.

Although much of the rest of the recapitulation is a transposition to the tonic of the original second subject and closing theme, there are many other subtle changes of this sort. For example:

➤ Had Mozart simply transposed the third bar of the second subject, labelled *(a)* in the example right, down a 5th, it would have appeared as shown in *(b)*. But instead he uses **octave displacement** to project the melody into a higher register, as shown in *(c)*. This is, in fact, the same type of modification that Mozart had used in the bassoon part of bar 64.

➤ Following a rescoring of the chromatic link in bar 249 (compare it with bar 61), the first violins' varied repeat of the second subject is now doubled by flute an octave higher, as well as by the bassoon an octave lower.

➤ In the exposition, the bassoon phrase beginning at bar 65^4 simply continues to double the first violins at the octave below, but at the corresponding place in the recapitulation (bar 253^4) Mozart introduces the oboe, which doubles the melody at the octave *above*. He also bolsters the accompaniment in this phrase with some quiet horn notes.

Make a detailed comparison of the instrumentation in the rest of the recapitulation with the corresponding bars in the exposition and see how many other differences you can identify.

A significant difference in structure occurs in the closing bars. The original codetta was ten bars long (bars 111–120). In the recapitulation, Mozart expands this into a 15-bar coda to emphasise the finality of the tonic key. This is done by inserting a short cadence figure (bar 305) before the demisemiquavers return and then by expanding the repeated G major harmony of bar 120 into a five-bar flourish that gloriously affirms C major. Listen out for the brass arpeggio four bars before the end: it is a thrilling conclusion.

Exercise 13

1. At the end of the development, how does Mozart indicate to the listener that the recapitulation is about to start?

2. Why is it necessary for the transition to be different when it occurs in the recapitulation?

3. In bar 81, Mozart introduced a chord of C minor. What chord did he use at the corresponding place in the recapitulation?

4. Give an example of octave displacement in the violin parts of bars 299–303.

Project work

Design a large graphic plan of the structure of this movement (use at least A3-size paper). Indicate each section of the sonata form with a series of blocks and show the following details:

➢ The subsections

➢ The key centres

➢ The locations of the main themes

➢ Whether each section is played tutti or by just part of the orchestra.

> If you've been working hard through all this analysis, take a break and listen to the exquisite slow movement before continuing.

Third movement

Structure

This movement is a minuet and trio, the most common form for the third movement of a symphony in Mozart's time.

The **minuet** is a moderately fast dance in triple metre. It originated in 17th-century France and became one of the most popular social dances in aristocratic circles. Minuets in symphonies and similar works are not intended for actual dancing, of course – they are simply movements that reflect the style of the dance, particularly in their rhythm and phrasing.

> This minuet, like many others, is labelled 'Menuetto' – a widely used word, but one that doesn't exist in any language! It is a long-standing error that arose from composers adding the ending of the Italian word *minuetto* to the German term *menuet*.

The **trio** is simply another minuet. Its name reflects the fact that early trios were composed in a three-part texture but this practice had lapsed by the late 18th century. At the end of the trio the direction *Menuetto D.C. al Fine* indicates that the minuet should be repeated da capo ('from the top') until the word fine ('finish') is reached. The custom nowadays is not to observe the internal repeats in the minuet when it comes round for the second time.

This pattern of minuet – trio – minuet creates a **ternary form** for the complete movement. Within this, each dance has its own structure – the first, the minuet, being in **rounded binary form**.

The difference between ternary and rounded binary form

Ternary form consists of three sections, arranged in the pattern ABA. The A section is self-contained – in other words, it ends in the key in which it began – and the B section provides a contrast.

Binary form consists of two repeated sections – ‖: A :‖: B :‖ – which are not greatly contrasted. The first usually modulates from the tonic to a related key (generally the dominant or the relative major) and the second usually modulates more widely before returning to the tonic. Each section depends on the other for completion and so is not self-contained.

> You could think of binary form like a pair of semi-detached houses: both are needed to make a complete building.

In rounded binary form, *some* of the opening music returns at the end of the B section, in the tonic key, in order to create a sense of completion. We could express rounded binary form as ‖: A :‖: BA^1 :‖. Although this looks similar to ternary form (ABA), the repeats and the modulation to the dominant at the end of the first A section confirm the binary structure.

Remember, too, that the B section in ternary form contrasts with the A section, whereas in binary form there is little thematic difference between the two sections because all of the melodic material tends to be based on the opening.

Minuet

The first section includes several features that are entirely typical of the Classical style:

Bars 1–16   Section A

> A melody-dominated texture with the tune clearly presented by the first violins and with other instruments accompanying

> Eight bars in the tonic followed by eight bars in the dominant

> Harmony based almost entirely on chords I and V of the tonic and dominant keys

> Balanced periodic phrasing, consisting of:

>> A four-bar antecedent in C major, ending with an imperfect cadence (bars 1–4)

>> A four-bar consequent in C major, ending with a perfect cadence (bars 5–8)

>> A four-bar antecedent in G major, ending with an imperfect cadence (bars 9–12)

>> A four-bar consequent in G major, ending with a perfect cadence (bars 13–16).

The first-violin motif in bars 1–2, with its falling chromaticism, permeates the movement. It leads to an imperfect cadence in bars 3–4 with a light accompaniment from brass and timpani. Notice how chord Ic extends throughout the first two beats of bar 4, forming a double appoggiatura, which resolves to chord V on the last beat of the bar.

Make sure you can distinguish between the F♯s in bars 1 and 6, which are chromatic (they are immediately cancelled by F♮ and the cadences are in C major) and the F♯s in bars 10, 12 and 15, which are part of G major, confirmed by cadences in that key.

This antecedent is repeated one step higher in varied sequence to form the consequent (bars 5–8). This time Mozart ends the phrase with a perfect cadence, mirroring bar 4 by using another two-beat double appoggiatura which resolves to the tonic chord on the last beat of the bar:

Notice how both this movement and the first begin by defining the key with four bars that progress from chord I to chord V, answered by four bars that progress from chord V to chord I.

The first eight bars are marked *p* and have a light, mainly two-part texture, with a sparse bass part and no woodwind. At bar 9 the dynamic changes to *f* and the tutti contrasts strongly with the first eight bars. Mozart jumps immediately into the dominant key at this point, confirmed by V^7–I in G major in bars 10–11 and supported by a dominant pedal on flute, oboes and horns.

The melody of bars 9–10 reuses the chromatic motif from the start of the movement (C♯ is now the chromatic note) but this time it is followed by detached falling 3rds (bar 10). Bars 9–10 are repeated exactly to form bars 11–12. Section A then ends with a four-bar phrase containing more falling 3rds (bar 14, repeated sequentially in bar 15) over the progression Ib–II^{7}b–V–I in G major:

Section A is then repeated.

Section B   Bars 17–59   Bars 17–24 form an eight-bar phrase with melodic material based on the chromatic motif from the start of section A. This is turned into a two-bar figure in which every interval is a semitone (bars 17–18) and which is then repeated in rising sequence in bars 19–20. The melody in the next four bars might appear to be new but its lowest notes actually maintain the chromatic scale shape:

The chromatic harmony of this passage is underpinned by a pedal that anchors the tonality to G. Above this, the melody is doubled a 3rd lower by second violins, and both violin parts are doubled at the higher octave by oboes. Added to this complex texture are inner parts for bassoons (the lower of which is doubled by violas) and a countermelody for flute that emerges in the last four bars.

In contrast to the rich texture of these eight bars, the short link in bars 24^2–26^1 is announced by horns and strings in bare octaves. It is based on the falling-3rds idea from bar 14, and is repeated **antiphonally** by woodwind and brass, supported by timpani.

The last note of the link overlaps with the start of the next phrase in bar 28. This sounds almost like the return of section A in the tonic key, rather earlier than expected. However, it soon turns out to be a development rather than a restatement of the opening. Mozart turns the innocent dance mood into something much more symphonic with the aid of some masterful counterpoint. Bass instruments imitate the appearances of the descending chromatic pattern, while the violas have a countermelody which is often in contrary motion to the tune and that is also picked out by alternate quavers in the second-violin part.

Note how much of this follows the outline of the A section: bar 28 has the theme descending from G (as at bar 1), bar 32 has it descending from A (as at bar 5) and bar 36 from D (as at bar 9). However, at this point Mozart needs to avoid the original cadence in the dominant, so he replaces the music of bars 13–16 with a new cadential phrase (bars 40–43) that ends in C major. Brass and timpani play a simple part in the second half of the first three four-bar phrases, and right through the last phrase.

After this tutti, the *p* phrase in bars 44–51 comes as quite a contrast, especially since it is scored entirely for woodwind in a high register. The texture is still contrapuntal – in fact, even more intensely so, since Mozart uses a technique called **stretto** (literally 'tightened'), in which the imitative entries come closer together than before. Entries of the chromatic motif occur in bar 44 (second oboe), bar 45 (first bassoon) and in bar 46 (first oboe). Two bars later the flute also joins in, completing the four-part contrapuntal texture. The eight-bar phrase is continuous, ending with a perfect cadence in bars 51–52 which overlaps with the start of the final section.

To round off the binary form, Mozart reuses the second half of the A section (bars 9–16), transposed into the tonic key and given some changes in orchestration (notably, fuller parts for brass and timpani). This means that the two sections of the minuet finish with essentially the same eight bars of music, section A ending in the dominant and section B in the tonic. This common practice is sometimes described as a **rhymed ending** and is another example of the type of balance so characteristic of the Classical style.

The whole of the second section is then repeated from bar 17 to bar 59 before continuing with the trio.

Trio

This is another C major minuet, although much shorter. To avoid confusion with the main minuet we will label its two repeated sections C and D. We could regard this as another rounded binary form, although you may feel it is closer to ternary form (see the box *right*). Remember that labels such as rounded binary and ternary are an aid to our own understanding – they don't represent fixed forms into which composers invariably forced their ideas.

Mozart begins with a joke – the trio starts with a perfect cadence which, if the conductor has maintained the pulse, could easily be mistaken for the end of the previous minuet. Mozart has put the cart before the horse, placing the cadence first and the melodic part of the phrase in bars 3–4! The quavers of the latter clearly refer to the descending chromaticism of the minuet, as shown *right*.

Notice how the delicate orchestration contrasts with the previous tutti – the cadence is scored for flute in a relatively low register, bassoons in their tenor register and second horn on the bass line. The first violin's quavers are doubled by first oboe an octave higher and delicately supported by staccato lower strings who complete the Vb–I–V progression.

This four-bar phrase is answered by a varied repeat of the same material (bars 64–67), the ending being adapted to finish with a perfect cadence in C major this time. Although the first section of binary-form movements in major keys usually end in the dominant, very short first sections (and this is only eight bars long) often remain in the tonic, as Mozart does here.

This C section is then repeated before continuing.

Although the two repeated sections of binary form are labelled with different letters, they do not usually contain *contrasting* ideas. Often all of the material derives from the opening bars, as happens in Mozart's minuet.

The structure of the trio is less clear. It resembles ternary form in that the first section is self-contained (it ends in the tonic) and the second is in a contrasting key. But the absence of a clearly contrasted theme for the second section is more like rounded binary form. In short, Mozart devises a hybrid of the two forms to suit his purpose.

If you need to identify the form of the trio in the exam, either interpretation of the form (rounded binary or ternary) should be valid, providing you give reasons for your choice. A really good answer might explain how and why either interpretation is possible.

Bars 60–67   Section C

Section D   Bars 68–87

Immediately after the repeat we are plunged into the dark world of A minor (the relative minor key) with an eight-bar phrase over a dominant pedal. The dynamic is f and the whole orchestra is playing apart from the timpani (whose pitches of C and G are of little use in this key).

There are few occasions in the *Jupiter* Symphony where Mozart makes use of minor keys. This phrase is like the sudden outburst of C minor at bar 81 in the first movement.

The first two bars of section D are a minor-key variant of the first two bars of section C – just what we should expect in a binary-form movement. However, just as the quavers in bars 61^3–63 seem to look back to the minuet, so the dotted minims in bars 68–71 seem to look forward to the opening notes of the last movement (turn the page in your score and see if you agree).

Thematic links between movements are rare in 18th-century symphonies, but they were to become increasingly common in the 19th century.

The second section starts over a dominant pedal (as did the second section of the minuet). Because of the pedal, a root-position chord of A minor is not heard in this passage, which ends in bars 74–75 with another reference to the opening of the trio. The urgency of these eight bars is enhanced by the articulation of the pedal by the brass, whose third-beat pairs of quavers relentlessly follow the second-beat quavers of the chords in the lower strings.

The rising semitone of bars 74–75 is repeated in bars 76–77 and then treated in falling sequence, the last two notes of which (flute, bars 80–81) are also the first two notes of section C^1 (the 'rounding off' of the rounded binary form). Underpinning this, Mozart uses the familiar device of a circle of 5ths to return to C major – and this progression similarly continues through to the first two bars of section C^1. The two techniques combine to create a seamless join that is typical of Mozart's imaginative ingenuity in his late works:

circle of 5ths

To round off the binary form, Mozart repeats the whole of the short section C in bars 80–87 with two small changes:

➢ The chords to accompany the string melody are now sustained rather than staccato, emphasising the finality of this passage

➢ Flute and first bassoon join in with an arpeggiated dominant 7th in bar 86 and then double the melody in octaves in the last bar.

Bars 68–87 are then repeated, after which the minuet is played again, almost always without repeats in modern performances.

Exercise 14

1. How does the viola part relate to the cello part in bars 9–12 of the minuet?

2. The timpani play on the first beat of bars 13, 14 and 16. Why are they silent in bar 15?

3. Explain the term stretto. Where does a stretto occur in the minuet?

4. Why is the minuet described as being in rounded binary form?

5. Complete the blanks in the following paragraph:

    The trio starts with a four-bar antecedent phrase that ends with a(n) .... cadence in the key of .... This is followed by a four-bar .... that ends with a(n) .... cadence in the same key. The F♯ in bars 62 and 66 is a .... note that does not affect the tonality of this passage.

6. How significant are dynamic markings in achieving contrast within the minuet and trio?

7. What are the significant rhythmic differences between the themes of the minuet and the trio?

Round off your work on the *Jupiter* Symphony by listening to the last movement, following it through with your score. It provides a splendid finale to the whole work. The important aspects of the first and third movements have been covered in this chapter, but it is a good idea to develop the habit of reading widely at A level, and so two sources of further reading are suggested on page 21.

Sample questions

In section B of the listening paper there will be two essay questions on the *Jupiter*, from which you must answer one. You will be allowed to refer to an *unmarked* score of the work in the exam. Here are some questions for you to practise, but first read the tips below on essay writing.

(a) In the first movement, compare and contrast bars 244–299 with bars 56–111.

(b) Show how Mozart creates a variety of contrasting moods in the first movement of this work.

(c) Discuss the textures used by Mozart in the minuet and trio.

(d) How do the minuet and trio reflect their origins as dance music?

(e) Describe how the motif in bars 1–2 of the minuet is used in the rest of the minuet *and* the trio.

(f) Explain what is meant by periodic phrasing, giving examples from this set work. How predictable is Mozart's writing in this respect?

(g) Show how Mozart achieves variety in his orchestration through the use of different combinations of octave doubling.

(h) How significant are (i) circle-of-5ths progressions and (ii) minor chords and minor keys, in the two movements that you have studied?

Essay writing

A good essay requires three things:

➤ An understanding of the question

➤ A clear, relevant and logical answer, with no digression

➤ A comprehensive range of evidence to support the points made.

It is essential to focus on the question. Common faults include attempting to write all you know about the piece, relevant or not, and offering a prepared answer that deals with some entirely different aspect of the music. Even if you offer a lot of accurate information, failing to answer the specific question will lose many marks. For instance, if you are asked to discuss Mozart's use of melody, you are unlikely to get marks for describing the texture or harmony of the music.

Spend a minute or two making a short list of important points to cover before beginning the essay and, once you have started, avoid digression. There is no need for opening paragraphs to set the scene, or to describe the composer's life or other works. Dive straight in and tackle the subject head on, with one paragraph on each of your main points. Round the whole thing off with a brief summary that refers back to the original question. If you find your essay starting like the one below, you have almost certainly got off on the wrong foot since you are not writing about the music itself:

> Mozart was born in 1756 at the start of the Classical period and he learned to play the keyboard when he was very young. His father organised concert tours around the courts and cities of Europe for the young boy, who amazed audiences with his prodigious talents. He wrote many piano sonatas, string quartets, operas and other works.

Essays that require you to 'discuss', 'consider' or 'evaluate' require informed judgements about the work. Simple description, such as listing keys and cadences, will produce a dull and inadequate essay. For a good mark you need to highlight matters of significance, and use your knowledge to interpret and explain the factual detail. Try to avoid personal opinions of a general nature, such as stating how much you like the piece – an essay is primarily a piece of technical writing. However, show that you know the effect made by each feature you mention: for example, 'Bar 81 forms a startling contrast because of the sudden change in dynamic, entry of the full orchestra and use of the first significant minor chord in the movement.'

It is best to avoid long sentences as they can easily become so convoluted that the point gets lost. Organise your material into a logical order and try not to have to keep adding extra points as asterisked footnotes or additions in the margin. Leaving a blank line between paragraphs will help clarity of presentation.

Vague statements such as 'the second subject is very tuneful' and generalisations such as 'Mozart was a master of counterpoint' are unlikely to receive credit. Instead, cite evidence from the music itself in order to illustrate each of your main points. For example, you could say 'Mozart's contrapuntal skill is evident in the imitative treatment of the minuet's simple opening motif in bars 28–35 and in the stretto that begins in bar 44.'

While references to specific bar numbers are essential, it should not normally be necessary to copy out musical quotations from the score of the *Jupiter* unless you want to lay them out in a particular way to illustrate your point. Quotations of what other people have written about the work are seldom worth including – the examiners want to know what *you* have to say about the music, in your own words.

A good way to test yourself is to read the score through in a silent room, imagining the music being played as you go.

While musical quotations should not normally be necessary in your essay on the *Jupiter*, they can be useful when answering questions on Area of Study 2, as examiners may not be familiar with the music you have chosen. However, all quotations must be relevant – just writing out a few bars of music to show that you have memorised them will not gain credit.

Section C: Area of Study 2

Early in your course a choice must be made for the topic to study for Area of Study 2. It has to be **one** from the following list:

➢ 2a: Choral music in the Baroque period

➢ 2b: Music theatre: a study of the musical from 1940 to 1980

➢ 2c: British popular music from 1960 to the present day.

In the exam you will not have access to scores of the works you have studied. There will be two essay questions on each topic, from which you have to answer **one**.

AQA does not stipulate which pieces to study for each topic. This book discusses a selection of suitable and readily available works – these may overlap with music you study in class or they could provide a reserve of additional pieces to help in your revision. Either way, these pages show you the kind of detail you need to know.

Because no specific pieces are set, the questions will be of a more general nature than those on the *Jupiter* Symphony. Nevertheless, you still need to focus *on the music itself* in your answers in order to get a good mark.

There are essentially two broad types of question the examiners may ask:

➢ The first is to ask you to write an informative programme note on, perhaps, two or three pieces you have studied

➢ The other is to ask you to comment on how one or more of the main elements of music (structure, melody, rhythm, harmony, texture and the use of instruments) was used in one or more pieces from your chosen topic.

If you are studying musicals, turn to page 59. If you are studying British popular music, turn to page 71.

Section C: Area of Study 2a

Choral music in the Baroque period

In music, the Baroque spans the period from about 1600 to about 1750. It was an age that saw the birth of opera and the rise of instrumental music, but choral music also flourished and was often composed on a grand scale, reflecting the magnificent Baroque palaces and churches of the age.

A clear and easy introduction to Baroque music is available in:

Baroque Music in Focus by Hugh Benham. Rhinegold Publishing, 2007. ISBN 978-1-906178-13-0

There is a very wide range of music you can study for this topic, both sacred (for the church) and secular (non-religious).

Sacred music includes settings of the Mass (the main service of the Roman Catholic church) and works used in church services, including anthems, psalms, canticles (such as the Magnificat) and sacred cantatas. It also includes settings of the passion (the story of Christ's last days on earth) and sacred oratorios (large-scale works on a religious subject, but designed primarily for concert use).

Technical terms in this first section will be explained over the next few pages.

Secular choral music includes odes and secular cantatas, often written for special occasions such as weddings, birthdays and other events of local importance.

Types of movement

Whatever works you study, it is important that your choice includes the following types of movement:

➢ **Recitative**: a relatively large amount of text, usually set in in a speech-like manner, and lightly accompanied by a cello with either harpsichord or organ; often followed by an aria

➢ **Arias**: solo songs, often accompanied by a small orchestra and sometimes featuring an instrumental solo called an 'obbligato' part (duets, constructed along similar lines, were also used)

➢ **Choruses**: movements for choir with orchestral accompaniment.

We will look at examples of all of these, drawn from the works of three well-known composers of the late-Baroque period (between about 1700 and 1750). However, you could also include the study of choral music from the earlier part of the Baroque period in the 17th century. Some famous examples include:

➢ Monteverdi: Vespers (1610)

➢ Schütz: Christmas Oratorio (1660)

➢ Purcell: Hail, Bright Cecilia (1692)

➢ Charpentier: Te Deum (1698/9).

Choirs and orchestras in the late-Baroque period

In the Baroque period, cathedrals, royal chapels and even some large churches maintained choirs to sing at the principal services, as some still do today. These were small all-male choirs, with boys singing the upper part(s). In some establishments, the choir was supported by an orchestra and elaborate musical settings were used, including sections for soloists as well as the full choir.

Choral music written for secular venues such as concert halls and theatres frequently included solo parts for female opera singers as well as men, with the choruses sung by all the soloists together with the boys and men from a local cathedral or chapel choir.

Almost all Baroque music includes a **basso continuo** part – a bass part to be played on a cello (and sometimes also on a double bass and/or bassoon) and from which accompanying chords were improvised on instruments such as the harpsichord, organ and lute.

By the 18th century, orchestras generally consisted of a small body of strings (first violins, second violins, violas and cellos, sometimes with a double bass doubling the cello part an octave lower) plus at least one chordal instrument (see *left*). There might also be wood-wind instruments, usually oboes and bassoons, but also sometimes flutes or recorders. Trumpets and timpani were often added if the music was of a grand or festive nature.

Conductors were not used in the Baroque period: performances were directed by the harpsichordist and/or leading violinist.

Baroque instruments were not identical in sound to their modern counterparts: woodwind instruments had far fewer keys and (as we noted when studying the *Jupiter* Symphony) trumpets had no valves. Instruments such as the clarinet and piano were invented towards the end of the Baroque period, but were very rarely used before the second half of the 18th century. Listen to recordings or performances of Baroque music played on period instruments to get an idea of the sound of a Baroque orchestra.

Music for study

The examples in the rest of this section are taken from choral works by three famous late-Baroque composers: Vivaldi, Handel and Bach. We'll begin by placing the music in context.

Vivaldi was born in the Italian city of Venice in 1678, where he became *maestro di violino* (master of violin) at an institution for abandoned children called the Pio Ospedale della Pietà (Devout Hospital of Mercy). Much of his music was written to be performed by the girls and women there, who were renowned for their musical talent. Vivaldi's fame today rests primarily on his concertos, which include the *Four Seasons*, but he also wrote operas and church music, including a much-loved setting of the Gloria.

Antonio Vivaldi (1678–1741)

The Gloria is the most joyful of the five texts normally set to music in choral settings of the mass – the principal service of the Roman Catholic church, which was said or sung in Latin before the 1960s. However, it is not certain that this work comes from a complete Mass setting – it is normally performed as a work in its own right since, at around 30 minutes, it is of substantial length. Like most of Vivaldi's music, it is a work that was forgotten after the composer's death until being rediscovered in the 20th century.

Vivaldi's Gloria was written for the Pietà, probably in around 1715, and it became a popular part of the repertoire there. Although the work includes tenor and bass parts, it is thought that these were sung by low female voices (possibly transposing the lowest notes up an octave where necessary) since mixed-voice choirs were not considered appropriate for church music at that time. However, there were plenty of men in the congregation, who used to flock to the church of the Pietà in the hope of getting a glimpse of the ladies performing the music from behind pierced screens!

Handel was born in Germany in 1685. As a young man he spent time in Italy, but he eventually settled in England, where he became one of the most celebrated composers of the age, often being called upon to write music for great state occasions. It was the craze for Italian opera that first brought Handel to London, where he wrote more than 40 operas. But later in his life, as the fashion for Italian opera waned, he turned to writing oratorios with English words. One of these is *Messiah* (1741), which has remained one of the most popular of all choral works to this day.

George Frideric Handel (1685–1759)

An **oratorio** is a substantial work for soloists, choir and orchestra. In Baroque times it was not thought appropriate to attend worldly entertainments – especially opera – during the holy season of Lent. Composers such as Handel therefore supplied oratorios that drew on operatic forms, but that were not performed in costume, or with scenery or acting. The words were usually (but not invariably) of a religious nature.

Messiah is Handel's most well-known oratorio, although it is not his most typical, being far less dramatic than the Old Testament biblical stories that he set to music in many of his other oratorios. *Messiah*, in contrast, recounts selective aspects of the life of Christ in a mainly reflective fashion.

Messiah is often performed in the Christmas season. If you are studying music from this work, look out for a performance near you in December.

The complete work consists of some 52 individual movements (arias, recitatives, choruses and so forth) and takes around three hours to perform in its entirety. It was composed in just 24 days of intensive activity during the summer of 1741 and first performed in Dublin the following year. Although its subsequent reception at the Covent Garden Theatre in London was initially unfavourable, by 1750 *Messiah* had come to be recognised as one of the greatest choral works and has been constantly performed ever since.

Other choral music by Handel that you might choose to study include his four Coronation anthems (one of which is *Zadok the Priest*) and *Dixit Dominus*, a dramatic psalm setting written when he was a young man in Italy.

Johann Sebastian Bach (1685–1750)

Bach was born in the same year as Handel but had a very different career. He never travelled beyond northern Germany and in his lifetime he was better known as a brilliant organist than as a composer. Like Vivaldi, most of his music was neglected after his death until it was rediscovered a century or more later (although much is believed to have been lost forever). Nowadays, Bach is widely regarded as being among the greatest of all composers.

For much of his career, Bach worked as a church musician and he spent the last 27 years of his life directing the music in the principal church of Leipzig. A key part of his duties was to provide a cantata with orchestral accompaniment to be performed during the main service on Sundays and church festivals – he composed well over 200 such pieces.

A **cantata** is rather like a mini-oratorio. Most of Bach's church cantatas are around 20 minutes in length and consist of about six movements – recitatives, arias and the occasional duet, framed by an opening chorus and a concluding chorale (a German hymn) – although 'solo cantatas', written for days when the choir was on holiday, don't have any choruses. For church festivals, Bach wrote cantatas of twice the normal length and with as large an orchestra as possible. These were performed in two sections, one before the sermon and one after.

Bach also composed a smaller number of secular cantatas which don't use chorale melodies. These were written for a variety of occasions, ranging from weddings to town council elections.

The chorale was fundamental to the Lutheran (protestant) tradition of northern Germany and Bach often wove traditional chorale melodies into more than one movement of the cantata. The words of his church cantatas usually consist of a poetic interpretation of the Bible reading for the specific Sunday or festival for which the work was written.

Wachet auf, ruft uns die Stimme (known as 'Sleepers, Wake' in English) is a cantata written in 1731 for performance on the last Sunday before Advent, a season that looks forward to Christmas.

Bach also composed larger-scale choral music, among which were settings of the passion – musical accounts of the suffering and death of Jesus, intended for performance on Good Friday. He wrote four or five such settings, but only two have survived. The first is the Passion according to St John, first performed in 1724. The other, on a larger scale, was the Passion according to St Matthew, first performed in 1727. Bach's passion settings are similar in length and format to oratorios although, like his cantatas, they incorporate chorales. In some respects they are more dramatic than Handel's *Messiah* since the characters in the passion story, even those of Jesus himself, are personified by the singers, whereas *Messiah* is essentially a reflective account.

Recitative

The function of recitative is usually to move the story along, whereas arias tend to reflect on the events that have happened – so the pairing of recitative and aria provides excellent contrast. There are two types of recitative:

➢ **Recitativo secco** ('dry recitative'), in which the flexible rhythms of the singer are accompanied with generally sparse chords played by the continuo instruments

➢ **Recitativo accompagnato** ('accompanied recitative'), in which a more melodic vocal line, with a stronger sense of regular pulse, is accompanied by a larger group of instruments.

The following excerpt (No. 19 from Handel's *Messiah*) illustrates several features of secco recitative:

The bass stave is the continuo part, which would be played on the cello and also used as the basis for improvising accompanying chords, probably on an organ or harpsichord. The symbols below this stave indicate the chords to play, expressed as intervals above the bass note. This is known as a **figured bass**. By convention:

➢ The chords are often played in a short detached fashion, despite being notated in long notes

➢ The final perfect cadence is usually delayed until after the singer has finished.

The upper stave is for a solo alto. Notice that all of the first three phrases follow a similar melodic contour. The vocal setting is **syllabic** (one note per syllable) and the melody is mainly **conjunct** (moving by step). The singer often ornamented the vocal line in accordance with the conventions of the day – the small staves show some possible ways in which this might be done. Keyboard players sometimes introduce their own decoration of the figured bass. For

Although figures have been supplied for every chord in this example, composers often supplied little or no figuring, instead relying on the musical context and the experience of the player to know which chords to play.

example, Handel leaves an inviting gap after the words 'leap as an hart' that a continuo player might fill with a pictorial flourish.

The movement also illustrates how fluid the sense of key can be in recitative, even in one so short as this. This is helped by the absence of root-position chords until the last two bars. The first phrase is harmonised in G major, the second in C major and the recitative then ends in A minor.

Compare Handel's recitative with the following, which is the start of the second movement of Bach's cantata *Wachet auf*. The vocal line in this secco recitative for tenor is **disjunct**. The wide leaps combine with the dissonance of chords over a tonic pedal to portray the excitement of the imminent arrival of Christ, who is depicted metaphorically by the poet as a heavenly bridegroom:

The 18th movement of Bach's St John Passion 'Er leugnete aber und sprach' ('But he denied and said') is a secco recitative in which we hear a tenor narrating the story, with interjections from Peter and a servant woman. Bach again makes use of dramatic leaps in the vocal line, illustrating the horror of Peter cutting off a person's ear by setting the word *Ohr* (ear) to a sudden high G♯.

At the end of this movement Bach adopts a more melodic, aria-like style known as **arioso** for the words 'and he went out and wept bitterly'. To express the mood of lament, Bach uses a **melismatic** setting (many notes to a single syllable) and repeats the words to new music to maximise their impact.

A similar moment later in the St John Passion occurs in No. 30, *Barrabas aber war ein Mörder* ('but Barrabas was a murderer') in which Bach illustrates the subsequent flogging of Jesus with a long and frenzied melisma.

The vocal part includes anguished leaps of a diminished 5th and a diminished 7th, below which the bass rises inexorably up a chromatic scale as the sense of grief intensifies, before sinking back chromatically to the resolution of a perfect cadence. And while the bass plods on in steady crotchets, the tenor part is tied over on many of the strong beats, producing a series of heart-wrenching suspensions.

The contrast between recitativo secco and recitativo accompagnato is vividly illustrated in No. 14 from Handel's *Messiah*. The first four bars ('There were shepherds abiding in the field') are secco recitative, set in a mainly conjunct style over a tonic pedal in C major. This leads to F major as high strings enter for seven bars of accompanied recitative ('And lo, the angel of the Lord'). The quietly arpeggiated violin parts build up a sense of suppressed excitement, while the triadic vocal line seems to be a distant fanfare to herald the angel's imminent announcement.

A second passage of secco recitative modulates rapidly through the sharp keys and then the violins return for another section of accompanied recitative, now in the bright-sounding key of D major and accompanied by shimmering semiquavers.

Handel places his top notes skilfully in this recitative: the first occurs in the second section, after an upward leap of a major 6th to a top G for the word 'Glory', and this is trumped in the final section by a thrilling top A, an effect immediately capitalised upon by the first appearance in the whole oratorio of trumpets, on the downbeat of the following chorus.

Arias

Almost all multi-movement choral works of the late-Baroque period include solo songs known as **arias** ('airs' in English). They offer the opportunity to explore a particular aspect of the text and they provide contrast between sections of choral singing.

The text of Vivaldi's Gloria is divided into 12 short movements, in which arias for the soprano and alto soloists (and one duet) are interspersed between the choruses. The work is scored for oboe, trumpet, strings and continuo. As in almost all liturgical music for the Roman catholic church, there is no recitative.

Movement 10 is a setting of the Latin words *Qui sedes ad dexteram Patris, miserere nobis* which, referring to Jesus, means '[He] who sits to the right of God the Father have mercy on us'.

It is written for solo alto accompanied by a three-part texture of strings (violins, violas and cellos) with continuo, and it illustrates several important features of the late-Baroque aria:

➢ The mood established at the start is maintained until the end, with no obvious contrasts. This adherance to a single mood, known as an **affection**, throughout a movement is a common feature of much late-Baroque music.

➢ Words and phrases in the text are frequently repeated (unlike in recitative, where the text is rarely repeated).

➢ The main vocal section is framed by substantial instrumental sections, parts of which also return between the phrases in the voice part. This type of structure is called **ritornello form** – the Italian word ritornello meaning a 'little return'.

Ritornello form was frequently used in concertos by Vivaldi and his contemporaries, but it also lent itself extremely well to arias because the returning instrumental passages provide short resting places for the solo singer. It is also a form well suited to longer movements because the sections between the ritornellos, known as **episodes**, can modulate, thus preparing the way for fragments of the ritornello to return in a variety of related keys before the music returns to the tonic key at the end.

This $\frac{3}{8}$ time aria in B minor has a lively, dance-like mood, despite its minor key. It opens with an energetic ritornello for strings and continuo, establishing the key with a series of V–I progressions. Notice how the harmonic rhythm (a crotchet on the tonic chord and a quaver on the dominant chord) helps give the aria its dance-like character. The repeated conjunct motif in octaves (bars 4–5) will play an important role throughout much of the aria.

The following phrase is sequential, built round a circle-of-5ths progression and features a prominent syncopated rhythm in the

Written as:

Sounds as:

V _____ ib _____ iv⁷ V_____

first-violin part (bars 8, 10, 12 and right through bars 14–19). The syncopation is enhanced by the rhythmic device known as **hemiola** in bars 20–21 and 25–26, in which the position of the chord changes give the impression that two bars of ⅜ have become one bar of ¾, as shown *left*. Before this, a Neapolitan 6th adds chromatic colour in bar 18 – this is a triad on the flattened supertonic in first inversion (chord ♭iib), which is a first inversion of C major in the key of B minor.

The table *below* shows how instrumental ritornellos alternate with vocal espisodes, modulating through the three keys most closely related to B minor before returning to the tonic at the end. What is not so easy to show is the way the motif first heard in bars 4–5 permeates the movement, appearing not only in the ritornellos but also in both the vocal part and accompaniment of most episodes, and injecting terrific rhythmic momentum to the music.

Bars	Section	Key	Comments
1–27	Opening ritornello	B minor	In the **tonic** key, details as described above
28–58	First episode	B minor → F♯ minor	Long tied note at start. Circle of 5ths in second phrase. Motif from bars 4–5 used in vocal part and accompaniment. Hemiola in bars 56–57
58–64	Short ritornello	F♯ minor	Bars 1–7, transposed to the **dominant**
64–80	Second episode	F♯ minor → E minor	First vocal phrase is mainly syllabic, second is mainly melismatic and based on a rising sequence. Hemiola in bars 78–79
80–84	Short ritornello	E minor	Bars 1–5, transposed to the **subdominant**
85–92	Third episode	E minor → D major	Single melismatic phrase based on material from bars 1–6, ending with hemiola
92–96	Short ritornello	D major	Bars 1–5, transposed to the **relative major**
97–131	Fourth episode	B minor	Bars 98–105 are a repeat of bars 28–35 and bars 124–130 are derived from bars 15–21. Hemiolas in bars 119–120 and 129–130
131–150	Final ritornello	B minor	Bars 8–27 of the first ritornello

Also listen to 'Laudamus Te' the third movement of Vivaldi's Gloria, which is a joyful duet for two sopranos, again in ritornello form.

When you listen to the aria, look out for changes of texture in the accompaniment, which ranges from busy three-part counterpoint to bare octaves. Vivaldi takes great care not to mask the solo voice, often using either just continuo or the violin and viola (without continuo) to support the singer in the episodes.

'He was Despised' is the second movement in part two of Handel's *Messiah* and is another alto aria, this time in the key of E♭ major. The words are adapted from the Book of Isaiah in the Bible.

It is in **da capo form**, the most common structure for the longest type of aria in the first half of the 18th century. As we discovered when studying the *Jupiter* Symphony, da capo means 'from the top' and implies repeating the opening section after a contrasting section. It is therefore a type of ternary (ABA) form and so provides much more opportunity for contrast than other types of aria.

An important feature of the da capo aria that you won't often see in a score, but that you are likely to hear in recordings that attempt to recreate the style of a Baroque performance, is decoration of the vocal line when the first section returns. In a solemn aria like 'He was Despised', most singers restrict themselves to discrete ornamentation, but a livelier aria might well be treated to exuberant improvisation, designed to display the singer's agility and top notes.

The first 49 bars form the A section, which Handel casts in ritornello form, modulating to the dominant at bar 21 and then passing through a wider range of keys before returning to the tonic.

The B section provides a marked contrast to the sorrowful mood of the A section. It is in C minor (the relative minor) and Isaiah's prophecy that Christ would be lashed is underpinned by a quietly insistent dotted rhythm that never ceases until the last two bars.

Listen carefully for the following features in the A section:

➤ The three-note falling figure played in 3rds (with a trill on the second note) in bar 2 – it is used throughout the A section

➤ The plaintive flat 3rd (G♭) and flat 6th (C♭) in bars 6–7

➤ The 3rds motif from bar 2 used by the violins to punctuate the vocal part in bars 9–12

➤ The imitation of the vocal part by the violins in bars 13–16

➤ The adaptation of bar 6 to the dominant key in bar 18, in which the flat 3rd and flat 6th are specifically linked to the word 'grief'

➤ The shortened ritornello in the dominant (B♭ major) in bars 20–23

➤ The modification of the 3rds motif in bars 25–27

➤ The replacement of earlier mainly short figures by sustained harmony in the accompaniment of bars 27^3–32^3 (can you spot a circle of 5ths in this passage?)

➤ The contrast between the warm sound of chord ii^7 for the setting of 'a man of sorrows' in bar 32 and the dramatic sound of a sustained diminished 7th for the same words in bars 36–37

➤ The use of just the continuo to accompany the last vocal phrase of the section in bars 46^4–48^1. This is a common feature of da capo arias, since singers would often improvise a decorative **cadenza** at their final cadence on the repeat (see *right*). The necessary pause in the accompaniment at this point is more easily managed by just the small continuo group than by the whole orchestra

➤ The final ritornello in the tonic (bars 43–49).

In the B section, listen particularly to the harmonic progressions. The bass moves up stepwise from tonic to dominant in bars 51–52, then down stepwise from tonic to dominant (bars 53–55). A circle-of-5ths progression starts in bar 55 and ends in bar 59, and after the dotted rhythms finally cease in bar 66 (note the dramatic silence), the B section ends with a perfect cadence in G minor.

Written as:

and ac - quaint - ed   with grief.

Might be performed:

and ac - quaint   -   -   ed with grief.

The vocal score of *Messiah* edited by Watkins Shaw (published by Novello) shows the type of ornamentation that might have been added to this aria by singers in Handel's day. The small notes in that edition are taken from two 18th-century manuscript copies of the work.

A common variant of the da capo aria can also be found in most editions to *Messiah*: the B section of the aria 'The Trumpet Shall Sound' ends with the instruction *dal segno* ('from the sign'). This is a direction to begin the repeat of the A section from the sign (𝄋) at the start of bar 29, thus cutting the lengthy opening ritornello when the A section returns.

Sometimes Handel could be much more adventurous with the da capo structure. In 'Why do the Nations so Furiously Rage Together?', another bass aria from *Messiah*, he totally dispenses with a repeat of the A section and instead plunges straight from the end of the B section into an angry chorus ('Let us Break their Bonds Asunder') that tonally fulfils the function of restoring the tonic key.

The bass soloist in 'The Trumpet Shall Sound' is partnered by an impressive part for solo trumpet, known as an **obbligato** – a term for an indispensable instrumental solo in Baroque music that is often as important as the vocal part.

Bach, who tended to use a greater variety of instruments than Handel, frequently included obbligato arias in his choral works and could be just as imaginative in his treatment of the aria as Handel. A particularly moving example is the alto aria *Es ist vollbracht* ('It is Finished'), movement 58 in the St John Passion. It comes at the point in the Passiontide story when Christ has, at the end of the preceding recitative, uttered his final words from the cross. The overwhelming despair of the moment is captured wonderfully by the viola da gamba obbligato. Aspects of the music contributing to this include:

> The viola da gamba, or viol, is a bowed string instrument with frets that was in common use before the violin family rose to prominence. Although the range of the treble viol is similar to that of the modern viola, it is held in an upright position resting on the lap rather than on the shoulder. Bach was one of the last composers to write for it before modern times.

➢ The very slow tempo (Molto adagio)

➢ The minor tonality (B minor)

➢ The plaintive timbre of the viol, which sounds a little like a muted viola

➢ The falling opening motif, which permeates the first section and which comes from the setting of the words *Es is vollbracht!* at the end of the preceding recitative

➢ The sparse texture (voice, obbligato and continuo).

After the opening ritornello the A section modulates to the relative major (D) for an abbreviated ritornello that starts in bar 10. The second vocal section modulates more widely, but a final short ritornello in bars 17^4–19 brings the A section to an end in D major.

The B section could hardly be more contrasting. As the poet looks forward to 'Judah's hero' turning death into victory, Bach:

➢ Changes from a slow quadruple metre to a fast triple metre

➢ Thickens the texture by adding the full string ensemble

➢ Remains largely in the bright key of D major

➢ Introduces broken-chord figures and energetic melismas into the vocal part.

But there are more surprises to come. This B section comes to an abrupt end in mid phrase on a diminished 7th chord in bar 40, and the unaccompanied alto soloist declaims 'It is finished' to an exact transposition of the motif first introduced by Jesus in the preceding recitative. A variant of the opening ritornello follows, displaced by half a bar. But the tragedy seems to overcome the singer, who can manage nothing more but a final restatement of 'It is finished', now fitted to the final cadence of the ritornello.

The sense of loss that dominated the A section has the last word in this imaginative reinvention of the da capo convention. The emotional impact is intensified by the lack of the expected da capo and the stark reportage of the tiny recitative that replaces it, just 1½ bars in length: 'And he bowed his head and departed'.

Baroque composers also used a shorter type of aria, known as a **cavatina**, which almost always maintained the same mood (or affection) throughout, without a contrasting section. These often resemble the first section of a da capo aria, moving from the tonic to a related key and then returning, perhaps via other keys, to the tonic – rather like a binary-form movement without repeats.

Handel again provides a good example in the aria 'But Thou Didst Not Leave his Soul in Hell' from *Messiah*:

➢ The opening ritornello is in A major

➢ The first vocal episode modulates to the dominant, with a cadence in E major in bar 14

➢ A short central ritornello (starting on the last quaver of bar 14) is a transposition to the dominant of the second half of the opening ritornello

➢ The second, longer, vocal episode modulates back to the tonic reaching a cadence in A major in bar 37

➢ The movement ends with a ritornello in the tonic that develops the second half of the opening ritornello.

This aria comes at a significant moment in *Messiah*: it is the first moment of joy about the resurrection after the prophecy of the crucifixion. There is therefore a spirit of confidence and optimism, achieved through the use of:

➢ A major key after previous movements in minor keys

➢ Mainly short vocal phrases which clearly define the tonality. For example, the first vocal phrase begins by outlining the tonic triad and ends with the progression I–V. The same pattern is repeated in the dominant in bars 174–193. Notice also the confident rising scale of E major that spans the interval of a 10th in bars 12–13

➢ A 'walking bass' in quavers that drives the music forward

➢ A clear, three-part texture formed from the vocal part, the instrumental melody (played by first and second violins in unison) and the bass part (in which the cellos are doubled by two bassoons in the ritornello sections).

Choruses

Movements 4 and 5 of Vivaldi's Gloria are clear examples of the two main types of texture found in Baroque choral music.

The first of these, 'Gratias agimus tibi', is a strictly **homophonic** (or **chordal**) setting in which all the parts, vocal and instrumental, move in the same rhythm like a hymn.

The second, 'Propter magnam gloriam', has a **contrapuntal** texture and is a **fugal** movement in which the subject announced by the sopranos in bar 1 is imitated by each part in turn. Notice how the initial rising 5th in the soprano and tenor entries becomes a rising 4th in the alto and bass parts, in order to avoid modulation in these opening bars. Entries of the fugal subject dominate the rest of the movement, including a **stretto** (see page 39) in bars 12–13. The choir is doubled by strings, Vivaldi ingeniously using the first violins to double the altos *an octave higher*, giving the impression of a countermelody above the soprano part.

Most choral movements include a variety of textures, as can be heard in 'Domine fili unigenite', movement 7 from Vivaldi's Gloria. This joyful chorus, with its infectious skipping rhythms, is another ritornello structure. Vivaldi uses various different pairings of voice parts when there is singing during a ritornello, reserving the full choir for contrast in the three episodes:

> The last movement of the Gloria is a **double fugue** (with two simultaneous subjects), which Vivaldi reworked from a movement in a Gloria by one of his Venetian contemporaries.

Bars	Section	Key	Comments
1–8	Opening ritornello	F major	Rising theme in violin 1 against descending scale in bass. Hemiola in bars 7–8. Cadence overlaps with start of …
9–17	Paired entry of altos and basses	F major	Varied repeat of ritornello followed by a one-bar link (bar 17) that modulates to the dominant
18–25	Paired entry of sopranos and tenors	C major	Varied repeat of ritornello in the dominant. Cadence overlaps with start of …
26–37	First episode: SATB in four-part counterpoint	F major → A minor	Circle of 5ths in bars 26–33. Sopranos and altos in canon at interval of 4th and distance of one bar. Prominent hemiola in bars 35–36. Cadence overlaps with start of …
37–40[1]	Shortened ritornello	A minor	Last note overlaps with start of …
40–53	Second episode: SATB in four-part counterpoint	A minor → D minor → B♭ major	Soprano melody in bar 40 is imitated by altos three bars later. Free counterpoint in tenor and bass parts. Hemiola in bars 51–52. Cadence overlaps with the start of …
53–61	Paired entry of tenors and basses	B♭ major	Ritornello in the subdominant followed by a one-bar link (bar 61) that modulates back to the tonic. Essentially a transposed and rescored repeat of bars 9–17
62–69	Paired entry of basses and tenors	F major	Ritornello in the tonic. The counterpoint of bars 53–61 is inverted so that basses now have the theme. Descending sequences over a circle of 5ths starting in bar 65
70–90	Third episode: SATB in four-part counterpoint	F major	Similar to first episode. Starts with SA in 3rds imitated by TB in 3rds over a circle of 5ths. Imperfect cadence in bars 77–78. Bars 79–84 are repeated to form bars 85–90
90–98	Final ritornello	F major	Repeat of first ritornello

In the opening ritornello, notice how the scalic ascent of the main theme runs in contrary motion to the descending diatonic scale in the bass. The chorus is in what Baroque musicians termed the French style, characterised by its persistent dotted rhythms. In performance the convention is to give these even more energy by playing them as shown *right*.

Written as: *Performed as:*   *or*

One of the most famous choral movements of all time is the Hallelujah chorus from *Messiah*. It is written in the grand style of Handel's Coronation Anthems, and includes a clear range of choral textures.

After a short introduction for strings and continuo (with bassoons), the choir's first eight-bar passage is confidently homophonic. The first half starts with the alternation of chords I and IV, the second with the alternation of V and I. The word 'hallelujah' is repeated ten times before any other text is used, Handel varying the position of the rhythmic accents to avoid any sense of monotony. Listen carefully (preferably with an orchestral score) to see how the upper strings fill the rests in which the choir breathes with motifs related to the choral parts.

The next line, 'for the Lord God Omnipotent reigneth' is set to an arch-shaped melody that rises stepwise from dominant to tonic and then returns by step to the dominant. Longer note lengths and a texture of bare octaves (for both choir and orchestra) adds grandeur to this simple idea. When the homophonic hallelujahs return, it is with the glittering addition of trumpets and timpani. Everyone initially has the 'hallelujah' rhythm, punctuated by quaver rests.

> The direction *tasto solo* ('single key') in bar 12 is a warning to the continuo keyboard player(s) not to wreck the effect of the bare octaves by playing chords in this passage.

These five bars are repeated in bars 17–21, this time starting and ending on the tonic. The 'for the Lord God' theme is then surrounded by the 'hallelujah' figure in free counterpoint, this section ending with plagal cadences in bars 32 and 33.

Eight bars of homophonic writing follow, in which the low vocal register of 'The Kingdom of this world' (for which trumpets and trumpets are silent) is dramatically answered by 'the Kingdom of our Lord' in a much higher register, supported by the re-entry of the trumpets and timpani.

Handel then introduces a new theme for the words 'and He shall reign for ever and ever', which is treated in fugal style (like the beginning of a fugue). This is interrupted in bar 51 by sopranos and altos on a monotone proclaiming 'King of kings and Lord of lords' (doubled by oboes), against which everyone else rhythmically hammers out 'hallelujah' and 'for ever' on chords I and V.

In the sort of thrilling passage for which he is justly famous, Handel then repeats this idea in ascending sequence, ratcheting up the excitement by starting the monotone on D (sopranos doubled by trumpets and oboes) and moving inexorably up the scale. Rhythmic interjections in the other parts continue against this sustained line. As the sopranos reach a top G, Handel's masterstroke is to delay the entry of lower parts in longer notes (bar 67) to produce an overwhelming sense of climax. But he is not finished yet and so uses an imperfect cadence in bars 68^3–69^1, which leads to …

A festive flurry of free counterpoint around the earlier fugue-like subject ('And he shall reign for ever and ever') starts in bar 69, followed by the 'King of kings' monotone (now allocated to the powerful sound of unison tenors and basses on D above middle C), which is again surrounded by 'hallelujah' rhythms.

The upper strings break into semiquavers as choral homophony returns. Bars 81–85 consist entirely of triumphantly rising figures against repeated tonic chords of D major. A final entry of the fugal subject appears in the bass at bar 85, after which the last seven bars consist entirely of chords IV and I. At the very end Handel uses one of his most famous fingerprints in this type of movement: a dramatic silence before the final (plagal) cadence.

The opening chorus of Bach's cantata *Wachet auf* is also on a grand scale, but it reveals how Bach drew more on the contrapuntal traditions of northern Germany than on the dramatic devices that made Handel's music so popular in England.

The movement is based on the chorale *Wachet auf* (Sleepers, Wake), which appears in a simple four-part setting at the end of the cantata. Before studying the first movement, familiarise yourself with this melody, which also appears in the tenor part of the famous fourth movement ('Zion hears her watchmen's voices').

> A cantus firmus (literally, 'held song') is a pre-existing melody, usually stated in long notes, that is used as the basis for a contrapuntal composition.

The opening chorus is a **chorale fantasia** – an extended movement based around a chorale melody. This melody appears as a **cantus firmus** in the soprano part, around which the orchestra and the rest of the choir weave intricate counterpoint.

It opens with a ritornello which introduces two ideas that will dominate the accompaniment – the French-style dotted rhythm of the bars 1–4 and the syncopated semiquaver figures that follow.

The cantus firmus starts in bar 17, supported by the dotted motif from the ritornello. Two bars later, the three lower voices introduce an imitative idea that fits not only with the continuation of the cantus firmus in the soprano, but also with the semiquaver motif from the ritornello that Bach uses in the accompaniment.

Bach uses a similar texture for the second line of the chorale (bars 29–39) but at the start of the third line (bar 43) the lower voices enter with the cantus firmus, proclaiming 'wake up, wake up' to rising intervals, before continuing with imitation at just one beat's distance, giving a sense of stretto.

All of this music is repeated (with the repeat being written out) for lines 4–6 of the chorale.

Following a ritornello that modulates to the dominant (B♭ major), Bach introduces the lower voices first in bar 117, the sopranos following in the next bar with line 7 of the chorale. This section is repeated (starting in bar 127) for chorale line 8.

Bach's treatment of the next section ('Allelujah', starting in bar 135) is perhaps the most remarkable. He creates a fugal exposition, based on the semiquaver motif from the ritornello, which is combined with the dotted motif in the accompaniment and, after 15 bars, with the next four notes of the cantus firmus.

The final lines of the chorale are set in a similar manner to the opening phrases, although with a more homophonic treatment of the lower parts in a few bars, and the movement ends with a repeat of its opening ritornello.

We have concentrated mainly on the choral writing, but the instrumentation is also important. Bach uses strings and continuo, plus a horn (which doubles the cantus firmus). There are also three oboe parts, the third of which is for a *taille* (a tenor oboe, similar in range to the modern cor anglais). In accordance with standard Baroque practice, one or more bassoons would normally have been added to the continuo group when oboes are playing.

Bach uses the oboes in **antiphony** with the strings at the start (see *right*) and adds suspensions for the first oboe above the first violin semiquavers in the passage that starts in bar 9. Such orchestral writing continues throughout the movement, even when the chorus is busy. Study the score while listening in order to make sure you can hear all that is going on; then just listen and enjoy.

Our final example is the chorus 'Lasset uns den nicht zerteilen' ('Let us not divide it'), movement 54 from Bach's St John Passion, in which the choir represents the soldiers at the foot of the cross bickering over who should have Jesus's robe. The densely packed contrapuntal entries of the subject, and its syncopated counter-subject, vividly portray the various factions squabbling while the cellos add to the agitation with an **Alberti bass** of almost perpetual semiquavers that cease only for the main cadences.

> An **Alberti bass** is an accompaniment pattern in which the notes of a chord are sounded in the order low, high, middle and high again. It is named after an early 18th-century composer who was rather addicted to the device.

The writing is essentially fugal: basses and altos start the subject on the tonic (C), while tenors and sopranos respond with the tonal answer starting on G. So non-stop is the argument that there is no other material and no episodes in the fugue.

No sooner is the fugal exposition in C major complete than the basses launch a new set of entries in the relative minor (A minor) at bar 8. The next set, starting in bar 15, is back in C major, where the voices enter in the order T–A–S–B. The fugue then modulates more widely, reaching a perfect cadence in E minor in bars 23^3–24^1. The movement surges on with more entries over a circle of 5ths:

Bars	24	25	26	27	28	29	30	31	32	33	34
Chords	Em E⁷	A	D	G	C	F	B♭	E dim	A	Dm	Gm
Entries	S	A	T	B		S	A	T	B		

Another structural perfect cadence, this time in D minor, occurs in bars 37^3–38^1, after which the entries resume on a succession of rising 4ths (bass D, tenor G, alto C and soprano F) and another circle of 5ths leads to the last section. With a touch of humour, the upper voices at last stop arguing and join together in three-part homophony in the final four bars, but the basses drag their heels until the final cadence before they, too, agree.

So frenzied is the choral writing in this movement, there is little need for independent orchestral parts. With the exception of the cello, both woodwind and strings double or shadow the voices.

Exercise 15

1. The vast majority of solos in Vivaldi's choral music are for female voices. Why is this?

2. Explain the difference between recitativo secco and recitativo accompagnato, naming an example of each from works you have studied.

3. Name four different instruments that might play a continuo part.

4. What is the opposite of melismatic word setting?

5. What is the most common structure for a late-Baroque aria?

6. Explain what is meant by 'obbligato'.

7. What is a chorale?

8. In a fugal movement, what device do composers sometimes use to increase the excitement of a set of entries of the subject?

9. Explain what is meant by a 'cantus firmus'.

10. What is an antiphonal texture?

11. What do you understand is meant by the term 'imitation'?

12. In what type of texture would you be most likely to hear imitation?

In section C of the listening paper there will be two essay questions on Baroque choral music, from which you must answer one. You will *not* have access to scores or recordings for this part of the exam.

Here are some questions for you to practise, but first make sure that you have read the tips about essay writing on pages 41–42.

Sample questions

(a) Explain what is meant by 'recitative', and describe some of the ways in which it is used in Baroque choral music.

(b) Show how Baroque composers used a variety of textures in their music for choir (do *not* include solo movements such as recitatives and arias in your answer).

(c) Discuss how instruments are used to accompany voices in Baroque choral music.

(d) Compare two choruses from the works that you have studied which you regard as making a dramatic impact.

(e) Explain what is meant by 'ritornello form' and describe how it is used in a Baroque choral movement of your choice.

(f) Show how Baroque composers used tonality as a structural device. Refer to at least two different works in your answer.

(g) Discuss the use of counterpoint in two contrasting movements from the works you have studied.

(h) Describe the variety of movements to be found in *either* an oratorio *or* a cantata of the Baroque period.

Section C: Area of Study 2b

Music theatre:
a study of the musical from 1940 to 1980

The history of musical plays, or 'musicals' as we now call them, goes back to the 19th century. By the 1920s they had become an immensely popular form of entertainment, particularly in New York and London. Many of these early musicals had a light romantic plot, with plenty of spoken dialogue, and include songs and dance numbers composed in the popular styles of the day. Exotic locations, with colourful costumes and scenery, also play an important role in many musicals – especially when film versions of stage musicals started to appear from the 1930s onwards.

The first two decades of the set period are often regarded as the golden age of the musical, and were followed by some inventive new approaches to the genre in the 1960s and 1970s. You therefore have an enormous choice of works to study. The list *below*, which is by no means exhaustive, includes some of the best-known shows of the 1940–1980 period. Excerpts from items marked with an asterisk (*) are discussed in the following pages.

> An account of the history and development of the musical, with a detailed study of key works such as *West Side Story*, is available in:
>
> *Musicals in Focus* by Paul Terry. Rhinegold Publishing, 2008. ISBN 978-1-906178-24-6

1943 * *Oklahoma!* (Richard Rodgers)
1944 *On the Town* (Leonard Bernstein)
1946 *Annie Get Your Gun* (Irving Berlin)
1948 *Kiss Me, Kate* (Cole Porter)
1949 *South Pacific* (Richard Rodgers)
1950 * *Guys and Dolls* (Frank Loesser)
1951 *The King and I* (Richard Rodgers)
1956 * *My Fair Lady* (Frederick Loewe)
1957 *West Side Story* (Leonard Bernstein)
1959 *The Sound of Music* (Richard Rodgers)
1960 *Oliver!* (Lionel Bart)
1962 *A Funny Thing Happened on the Way to the Forum* (Stephen Sondheim)
1964 *Hello, Dolly!* (Jerry Herman)
1964 * *Fiddler on the Roof* (Jerry Bock)
1966 *Cabaret* (John Kander)
1968 *Joseph and the Amazing Technicolor Dreamcoat* (Andrew Lloyd Webber)
1971 *Godspell* (Stephen Schwartz)
1971 *Jesus Christ Superstar* (Andrew Lloyd Webber)
1973 * *A Little Night Music* (Stephen Sondheim)
1973 *The Rocky Horror Show* (Richard O'Brien)
1975 *A Chorus Line* (Marvin Hamlisch)
1975 *Chicago* (John Kander)
1976 *Annie* (Charles Strouse)
1978 * *Evita* (Andrew Lloyd Webber)
1979 *Sweeney Todd* (Stephen Sondheim)
1980 *Les Misérables* (Claude-Michel Schönberg)

> Useful information about these and many other shows can be found on www.broadwaymusicalhome.com which has links to download songs from many shows on iTunes.

Choosing what to study

Aim to study songs and shows by a range of composers from the 1940–1980 period and include examples of all of the main genres (solo songs, duets, ensembles, choruses and dances). Try to include songs in contrasting moods that come from the same show.

The extracts discussed in this book have been chosen from the six shows summarised below. All of these are available on DVD, but be aware that film versions of musicals are often signficantly different from the stage shows on which they were based.

Oklahoma!

Oklahoma! was the first collaboration between two writers who had already achieved great success on Broadway – Richard Rodgers, who wrote the music, and Oscar Hammerstein II, who wrote the words. It opened on Broadway in March 1943 and ran for over 2,000 performances. *Oklahoma!* has been re-staged many times since and the 1955 film version of the work is available on DVD. It was particularly influential for the way in which songs and dances form a logical part of the script (known as the 'book' in musicals), and is therefore often described as a 'book musical'. The story revolves around the disputes between cowboys and farmers in early 20th century America, with both drama and romance in the plot.

Guys and Dolls

Frank Loesser wrote both the music and the song lyrics (but not the book) for *Guys and Dolls*, which opened on Broadway in 1950, playing for 1,200 performances. The story concerns a bet between Nathan Detroit and Sky Masterson over whether Sky can make the next girl they see fall in love with him. The next girl happens to be Sarah Brown of the Save-a-Soul Mission; suffice to say, Sky wins the bet. The 1955 film version of the show, starring Marlon Brando, Jean Simmons and Frank Sinatra, is available on DVD.

My Fair Lady

With music by Frederick Loewe and words by Alan Jay Lerner, this is one of the most highly regarded of all musicals, *My Fair Lady* ran for 2,717 performances on Broadway when it opened in 1956, and is adapted from George Bernard Shaw's play *Pygmalion* (1913). Professor Henry Higgins, an expert in dialects, makes a bet with his friend Colonel Pickering that he can take a flower girl from Covent Garden market and coach her to speak so well that she could pass as upper class. With scenes such as the races at Ascot and the Embassy Ball, this show is both a musical and visual treat. The 1964 film version is available on DVD.

Fiddler on the Roof

Set in a Jewish village in Russia, *Fiddler on the Roof* centres on the dairyman Tevye and his attempts to maintain old traditions as his daughters grow up in a changing world. Jerry Bock's score captures the spirit of traditional Jewish music, with such famous songs as 'If I were a Rich Man'. First staged in 1964, the work ran for 3,242 performances on Broadway. The award-winning 1971 film version is available on DVD.

A Little Night Music

Stephen Sondheim, who wrote the lyrics for Bernstein's *West Side Story* (1957), is a composer as well as a lyricist, and one of the most important figures in the recent history of the American musical. *A Little Night Music* is a sophisticated work (the title derives from a famous work by Mozart) and is based on an Ingmar Bergman film. It is a romantic comedy, set in late 19th century Sweden, about a group of people spending a weekend in the country. Much of the score, which includes Sondheim's most well-known song, 'Send in the Clowns', is influenced by 19th-century waltz music. *A Little Night Music* opened on Broadway in February 1973. The 1978 film version is available on DVD.

First staged in 1978, *Evita* tells the story of the life and death of Eva Perón, a singer from small-town Argentina who travelled to the capital, Buenos Aires, and fell in love with Colonel Juan Perón, soon to become president. The rags-to-riches girl never forgot her roots, starting the Eva Perón Foundation to help Argentina's poor, and inspiring devotion and affection from her people. The hope was never fulfilled: Eva died of cancer at the age of 33, and the political history of Argentina in the second half of the 20th century was not to be a smooth and happy one. The work was something of a departure for lyricist Tim Rice and composer Andrew-Lloyd Webber, whose two best-known earlier musicals had been based on the Bible, but it sped Lloyd-Webber on to many further hit shows, written with other lyricists, in the years that followed.

> Lloyd-Webber's later musicals, such as *Phantom of the Opera*, fall outside the dates for this topic set by AQA.

Song form

In the first part of our period, composers continued to favour **32-bar song form**, the most common structure used in popular songs since the 1920s. Essentially 32-bar song form consists of four eight-bar phrases, in the pattern AABA or AABA[1]. However, it is a potentially confusing term because:

> ➢ The 32-bar format refers only to the **chorus** of the song – there are almost always other sections, such as verses

> The term 'chorus' here refers to the refrain of the song – not necessarily a section that is sung by a chorus.

> ➢ Phrases (particularly the last) may be longer than than eight bars and/or may be used in a different order, such as ABAB.

'The Surrey with the Fringe on Top' from *Oklahoma!* shows how 32-bar song form is used in practice. It consists of:

➢ Verse 1 (four similar four-bar phrases)

➢ Chorus 1, comprising:

> ➢ An eight-bar phrase (A)

> ➢ A repeat of phrase Λ to different words

> ➢ A contrasting eight-bar phrase (B)

> ➢ A repeat of the first phrase, extended to 12 bars for a more conclusive effect (A^1)

➢ A second verse and chorus, using the same music as the previous two sections, but with different words and different singers

➢ An instrumental interlude over which there is spoken dialogue

➢ A third verse and chorus, using the same music as before, but slower and with different words.

The chorus suggests the image of a Surrey (a horse-drawn carriage) with persistent rhythms to suggest the clip-clop of horses' hooves. Its A phrase is constructed in the pattern 2 bars + 2 bars + 4 bars. Each of these units starts with a bar of repeated crotchets on the dominant, with an upward leap in the next bar that gradually gets wider: up a 4th to A in the first unit, up a 5th to B in the second, and up a 6th to C♯ in the third unit. It is this final leap of a major 6th that creates the momentum for this third unit to continue for four bars in order to reach a cadence.

> Notice how the sustained falling scale in the accompaniment of the chorus contrasts with the staccato of the other parts. Simple countermelodies like this were a favourite device of composers of the period.

The music of the first two A phrases is almost identical. They both end with an imperfect cadence, but in the first the singer finished on a low E while in the second he finishes on a high E.

The B phrase consists of two four-bar units which are similar, but the second involves a brief modulation to the dominant, ready to return to A major for the final A phrase. This is extended in order to reach a perfect cadence in which the singer ends on the tonic.

Composers were able to achieve all manner of variety within 32-bar song form. Frank Loesser in *Guys and Dolls*, for instance, changed the metre and tempo of the B phrase in 'Take back your Mink' in order to capture Adelaide's imperfect attempt to maintain her dignity as she takes a high moral stance. Later in the same show, in 'Luck be a Lady', Loesser portrays the excitement of Sky at the crapshoot by moving up a semitone for the second A phrase, and another semitone for the B phrase, before returning to the original key for the final quarter (each phrase in this song is 16 bars long with a 4+4+8 internal structure).

Solo songs

'I Cain't say No!' from *Oklahoma!* is sung by Ado Annie, a girl who gets into all sorts of trouble because she can never say no to the men in her life. There is a simple overall structure:

➢ Introductory verse

➢ 64-bar refrain

➢ Middle section (labelled 'trio' in the score)

➢ Refrain repeated with different words.

The opening verse underlines Annie's indecisive temperament by alternating bars of $\frac{4}{4}$ crotchets with $\frac{2}{4}$ quavers, and by contrasting a unison texture at the start of the first two $\frac{4}{4}$ phrases with a homophonic texture in their second halves. The verse is joined to the following refrain by a short link.

The refrain is an elongated variant of 32-bar song form: AABBA[1] in which the final phrase is extended to 24 bars.

The main idea is high spirited, beginning with **syncopation** in the melody and the crisp sound of a snare drum on the off beats. The accompaniment consists of four bars of diatonic harmony in an 'oom-pah' (or 'vamp') style. The same chords are repeated beneath a different melodic contour to form the second half of the A phrase.

When the A phrase is repeated (with different words) it ends more conclusively on the tonic rather than on the dominant. The eight-bar B phrase is also repeated with different words. There is a touch of raunch here, with a swooning chromatic line in the accompaniment and flirtatious acciaccaturas in the violins. Listen out for the splashes of woodwind colour here, too.

A colourful harp glissando leads to the final section, in which phrase A is extended from eight to 24 bars in order to incorporate some chromatic harmony on the way to a climactic final perfect cadence.

The middle (or trio) section is rather more sultry: Rodgers returns to quadruple metre, with a somewhat swung rhythm and ends on the dominant, ready for the return of the entire refrain. This has different lyrics but the same music, and it completes a highly successful and compact song, which, coming early in Act 1, gives the show great momentum.

'Send in the Clowns' from Sondheim's *A Little Night Music* is a totally different type of solo song. Whereas 'I Cain't say No' is a comedy number, Sondheim's famous **ballad** is imbued with mellow nostalgia. It comes near the end of *A Little Night Music*, at the point when the actress Désirée Armfeldt admits that she has failed to tempt a former lover back to her arms.

> A ballad is a slow solo song – often a love song or, as here, a reflection on events that have taken place.

An introduction for unaccompanied clarinet anticipates the first phrase of the vocal melody. The last note is harmonised with a tonic chord of Db major, played by the tender, warm sound of muted strings, supported by gently rippling harp arpeggios.

The song itself follows an AABA structure, although the phrases are of irregular length, with several changes between quadruple and triple metre. The first A phrase, despite its occasional leaps, is essentially arch-shaped, starting and ending on the low dominant with the upper dominant in-between. Listen for the pause and momentary break in accompaniment on the line 'you in … mid-air' – it returns several times with different lyrics and is something of a feature of the song. The second A phrase is adjusted to end more conclusively on the tonic and includes a fragmentary counter-melody in duplets for flute and clarinet.

The B phrase gathers a little momentum and starts in F minor (the mediant), which generates more intensity of feeling. There are a few chromatic twists in the harmony towards the end of this passage. The final A phrase is extended by two bars.

The clarinet returns with a link, which is essentially the A phrase, this time accompanied, above which there is some brief spoken dialogue with Fredrick. Désirée then appears to start a second verse but, almost as if she cannot bear to continue, it gets no further than a single statement of the A phrase, after which it ends with a delicately scored tonic chord on high strings, with the clarinet left (in mid-air?) on the 5th of the triad. The effect seems to capture the fragility of Désirée's hopes.

'On this Night of a Thousand Stars' comes early in Act 1 of Andrew Lloyd Webber's *Evita* and is in the style of a tango, the national dance of Argentina. It originated in the bordellos of Buenos Aires, and its overt passion and bittersweet flavour give the dance a strong and unmistakeable character. Aspects of this song that reflect the tango tradition, some of which are shown *right*, include:

➤ $\frac{4}{4}$ time with strong downbeats that are often prefaced with an anticipatory 'snarl' in the bass

➤ Triplet crotchets (a) and syncopated quavers (b) in the melody

➤ A dotted 'habañera rhythm' in the bass (c)

➤ The I–II⁷–V⁷–I chord progression (G–Am⁷–D⁷–G)

➤ The scoring for violin (in a low register), guitar, double bass, piano and bandoneón (a type of accordion with buttons rather than keys). These are all instruments of the traditional *orquesta típica* of tango music.

Although written near the end of our period, the conventional structure of the main part of this song should be apparent: it consists of eight-bar phrases in the pattern AABBA.

The A phrases are diatonic and end on the tonic. Some chromatic colour creeps into the B phrase (notably with the substitution of the minor version of chord IV when it comes around for the second time) and the characteristic habañera rhythm becomes much more persistent in this section.

At the end of the second B section, Lloyd Webber plays with his audience's sense of expectation by repeating just the opening three notes of the A section before the full phrase is heard. The fragment is echoed in the band by two Latin-American instruments, firstly the guitar and secondly the bandoneón.

Duets and ensembles

Duets in musicals are often expressions of love and 'Do You Love Me?' from *Fiddler on the Roof* is no exception, but it has a charming twist. During the course of a long marriage, Tevye and Golde have suffered all sorts of hardship, not least their daughters wanting to marry men they love rather than partners who have been chosen for them. Bewildered, Tevye asks his wife, 'Do *you* love *me?*'.

The question only needs four notes but they are perfectly chosen: a rising phrase with an accented passing note on 'love'. The reply promises to match, but there is a striking and unexpected leap of a major 6th in Golde's 'Do I *what?*' reflecting her surprise at being asked such a question after 25 years of marriage. So Tevye tries again: same question, same musical phrase. This time Golde is curious and gives a chromatically inflected response (see *left*).

This interchange of melodic fragments is actually the start of the A section of a standard song form. Golde continues over a spiced-up circle-of-5ths progression containing some wonderful chromatic touches in the accompaniment, before coming to the conclusion that her husband has indigestion.

Tevye tries again: the second A section. The music is much the same (just a few differences in the vocal line) giving Golde another chance to try and deflect the question.

The B section is primarily Tevye's: he recalls their wedding day and there are overtones of the ceremony in the narrow-range melody (reminiscent of Russian chant), parallel 3rds between melody and bass and the use of the tonic minor key. Then, as Tevye remembers how his parents told him that he and his new wife would learn to love each other, the austere harmony melts into another circle-of-5ths progression.

Tevye tries one more time: the final A section. And at last Golde admits that she probably does love her husband. Tevye makes a similar confession. A brief coda follows in which the husband and wife sing together for the first time – initially in unison and finally in sonorous 3rds.

'I Could Have Danced All Night' from *My Fair Lady* is an ensemble involving four singers. After a long day's work, Eliza, driven hard by Professor Higgins to lose her Cockney twang, has finally made a breakthrough. She is much too excited to go to bed and imagines herself dancing at a society ball in 'I Could Have Danced All Night', the rapidly pulsating accompaniment to which perfectly portrays her exhilaration.

At first it seems that this will be a solo for Eliza, who sings a brief introductory verse ('Bed! Bed! I couldn't go to bed!') followed by a refrain. The latter is in 32-bar song form (AABA) in which the second A phrase is a sequence of the first, up a step. The B phrase starts in the mediant key of E major but ends on the dominant of the home key (C major), ready for the return of the last A phrase, the last part of which is changed to include a climactic top F.

An eight-bar link (known as a **middle eight**) incorporates a short passage for two maids, after which Eliza repeats the refrain while Mrs Pearce (the housekeeper) and the maids provide a mildly impatient countermelody in the three A sections. This consists of short motifs in quavers, each energised by starting on the second quaver of the bar, and contrasts most effectively with the many long, legato notes in Eliza's aspirational melody. Listen for the isolated word 'please' in the maids' tune: it comes twice near the end of the first A section, all by itself on the final quaver of the bar, quite short and brittle, suggesting just a little terse irritation with the heroine.

Mrs Pearce almost has the last word at the end of this refrain, but Eliza has one more chorus – now on her own – which starts very quietly but builds up to finish on a long and brilliant top G as the curtain falls at the end of the scene.

Our next example comes from *Guys and Dolls*. Since much of this musical is concerned with the bet between Sky and Nathan, it is appropriate that early in the show there is a scene for three punters betting on horses. 'Fugue for Tinhorns' starts with a trumpet playing a mock hunting call over an 'oom-pah' accompaniment that runs through most of the number. Inevitably each man has a different opinion as to which horse is the sure bet, and this is superbly captured in the song which is constructed as a **round**.

> Tinhorns are gamblers who pretend to be wealthier than they really are. This pretentiousness is nicely reflected in the title of the number, which is not actually a fugue at all, but merely a humble round.

Nicely-Nicely is the first man to nail his colours to his chosen mast: he's going to put his money on a horse named Paul Revere. Nicely first sings the complete 12-bar melody by himself. Note how it is harmonised by a chord pattern that repeats as an **ostinato**. This is the device that helps the melody to work as a round – all three of its four-bar phrases use the same chord progression and all three fit together when sung simultaneously.

Notice how the first four bars of the tune contain syncopation and chromatic inflexions, whereas bars 5–12 are much simpler, some containing just two notes. As the round builds up, these simple bars will allow the more intricate material to be heard more clearly when both are sung at the same time.

In due course Benny, who is going to bet on Valentine, and Rusty, who fancies his chances with Epitaph, join in and Loesser keeps his round going for some while. The following chart shows where each man sings the melody:

The accompaniment keeps ticking over until bar 50, when the band interrupts the punters with a loud off-beat dissonance. This brings the men together: they are all now of one mind, each certain that their horse will win, they just disagree on which horse!

The final perfect cadence, like most of the musical, echoes the style of big-band jazz. A complex chromatic chord is substituted for the dominant while the tonic triad (sustained by the singers) is fleshed out with jazzy syncopated figures in the accompaniment.

Chorus numbers

Some songs consist of solo verses followed by choral refrains. One such example is 'Sunrise, Sunset' from near the end of Act 1 in *Fiddler on the Roof*. The Jewish community has gathered for the wedding of Tevye's daughter and forms the chorus which sings the refrains in response to the soloists' verses.

Golde and Tevye have the first verse of this minor-key waltz song. It has a simple, folk-like structure to suit the context: three similar four-bar phrases (the last of which is transposed up a 4th) followed by a four-bar cadential figure. These 16 bars are repeated with a varied ending to form the second half of the verse.

A dominant 7th at the end of the verse leads straight into the refrain, which has an ABAB structure of four eight-bar phrases. It starts with the men of the chorus who, following Jewish custom, form a separate group from the women and who harmonise the melody in parallel root-position triads. Bars 1–8 are based on tonic and dominant harmony, while bars 9–16 follow a circle-of-5ths progression. Female voices respond by repeating the refrain in two-part harmony.

Verse 2 involves more solo characters but is sung to the same music as the first verse. The refrain is then sung by the full chorus in a rich five-part texture. The second half sees an expressive counter-melody on the violins above the chorus.

In the final perfect cadence, there is a pause on the unaccompanied first chord, which has a plangent minor 3rd (B♭) in the melody above a dominant 7th (D^7) in the lower parts, after which the number ends in its resolutely minor key.

The chorus is often used to represent various different groups of people in the story during the course of a show. In *My Fair Lady* their roles range from cheerful cockney friends of Eliza's father to wealthy race-goers at Ascot. Strictly speaking, there is no need for a chorus in the scenes set in Professor Higgins's study, but the writers introduced (at a late stage in the creation of the work) a small chorus of six servants who, in 'Poor Professor Higgins!', comment on the action and convey a sense of time passing – time during which the Professor has worked ceaselessly to achieve his goal (and evenetually to win his wager).

The servants start with a dotted rhythm for the title words in a phrase that features a falling diminished 4th. They sing in four-part close harmony, with added major 6ths on chord I and minor 7ths on chord V (shown *right*). This is repeated and extended into a rising phrase of plain crotchets, after which 'Poor Professor Higgins' is sung in bare octaves to a new idea that spans the interval of a diminished 5th.

The servants then describe the professor's toil in a hymn-like section of crotchets and minims, based on a bell-like motif in which Loewe recalls the chimes of Big Ben to convey a sense of time passing. As the lights go down on the chorus, the Professor and Eliza are seen hard at work to the accompaniment of more chime-like figures. Two more verses follow, each transposed up by a semitone to increase the tension. In the last of these verses the words are changed to 'Quit, Professor Higgins!', which Loewe responds to by replacing close harmony with bare octaves for the singers. The chorus ends with chimes, now distant, as Eliza's lesson continues.

Many musicals include spectacular **production numbers**, often at the start or end of an act (the latter usually called the **finale**), involving the full cast – principals, chorus and dancers. One of the innovative aspects of *Oklahoma!* was the decision to place its famous title song almost at the end of the show, at the point when audiences would least expect anything new.

The song celebrates the imminent marriage of the show's two leading characters and the end of the animosity between ranchers and farmers as the news arrives that the territory in which they live is about to become the brand new American state of Oklahoma. It starts in something of a country style, with open strings on the violins to the fore and a rustic 'oom-pah' pattern. A short verse section includes a patchwork of soloists and, in the 24 section, a suggestion of a **hoedown**.

This leads straight into the main part of the song ('Oklahoma where the wind comes sweepin' down the plain') sung first by Curly as a solo. Although it consists of eight-bar phrases, there are rather unusually seven of them, in the order $ABAB^1CDE$.

The music then winches up a semitone, and a four-bar link leads to the entry of the chorus. They sing in harmony, involving up to seven parts in places. The texture is mainly homophonic, although the girls start by sustaining the first syllable of 'Oklahoma' in three-part harmony while the boys continue with the tune, and

A hoedown is a square dance (a type of folk dance) in duple metre that often featured in barn dances in rural parts of America in the early 20th century. The opening chorus in the second act of *Oklahoma!* ('The Farmer and the Cowman should be Friends') is a longer example.

later they have rising three-part scales against the sustained tonic opening of the tune sung by the lower voices.

At the end of the C phrase, Rodgers winds up the excitement by adding an extra passage – a rising chromatic scale in the upper parts over a dominant pedal in the bass, all sung to repeated cries of 'Yippy! Yi!'. The final two phrases lead to a **coda**. This starts with a steady crescendo, with repeating quavers in the bass (descending from tonic to dominant) over which the chorus gradually build up a dominant 7th chord to fragmented syllables of 'Ok-la- … -ho-ma'. The final phrases of the song then return one more time before the full company spell out the letters O-K-L-A-H-O-M-A and end with a high-spirited whoop of 'Yeow!'.

Overtures and dance numbers

The potpourri ('mixture') overture and the waltz song are among several features of 19th-century comic opera that were adopted by writers of early musicals.

Many musicals begin with an overture before the curtain rises. The most popular type is the **potpourri overture**, which consists of a medley of tunes from the show. The composer may also write **play-out music**, again based on songs from the show, to send the audience on their way after the final curtain, and **incidental music** to be played during scene changes.

Dance has played an important role in musicals throughout the history of the genre. In some cases, dancing arises naturally out of the action, such as the Embassy Ball that Eliza is taken to in *My Fair Lady* or the barndance in the second act of *Oklahoma!*

Some of the most famous uses of dance in a musical occur in Bernstein's *West Side Story*. It starts with a prologue in which the rivalry of the street gangs who dominate the work is conveyed in mimed action to music. It includes a series of 'challenge dances' between the gangs in 'Dance at the Gym' and the tragic ending of the work is enacted to music without any singing. In addition, many of its famous songs are based on Latin-American dance rhythms, and move fluently between song and dance.

In other cases, dance is used as medium for conveying ideas that cannot easily be expressed in dialogue or song. For example, instead of ending the first act of *Oklahoma!* with a rollicking production number, Rodgers and Hammerstein opted for an innovative ballet sequence in which dancers act out a dream that the intended wedding will turn into a nightmare, with Curly killed by his rival, Jud, who then abducts the bride. This premonition stays with the audience throughout the second act and very nearly turns out to be true when Jud arrives at the wedding with a knife … except that it is not Curly who is killed in the final minutes of the show.

In *Guys and Dolls* (which, like *West Side Story*, starts with action mimed to music) part of Sky's strategy for wooing Sarah, and thereby winning his bet, is to take her to Havana in Cuba. This allows Loesser to introduce a distinctly Caribbean flavour towards the end of Act 1, with an extended dance scene entitled 'Havana'. Its various sections, nearly all instrumental, are:

➤ The Café Cubano Shango

➤ The Polite Rhumba

➤ Tango

➤ Samba

➤ Rhumba.

Listen out for aspects of the music that reveal the Latin-American style of these dances. They include:

➤ The instrumentation, especially Latin-American percussion

➤ The various syncopated dance rhythms, especially the grouping of eight quavers into the pattern 3+3+2

➤ The extent to which the harmony depends on chords I and V, with phrases starting over chord V

➤ The use of different registers for melodic variety.

Much more formal styles of social dance occur in *My Fair Lady*, which is set in the Edwardian London of 1912. The ball scene, featuring the 'Embassy Waltz', has already been mentioned, but before this Eliza is taken to the races at Ascot in a scene that opens with a chorus in the style of a gavotte. Whereas a waltz is exactly the sort of music that would be heard at a ball in 1912, a gavotte (a long-dead dance from the 18th century) is the last thing you would expect at a race meeting!

In fact, Loewe is taking the opportunity to poke fun at the upper-crust English society whose speech Eliza is trying to emulate (none too successfully when she lets slip some lurid cockney swearing at a critical moment). The chorus leads into a parody of an 18th-century gavotte – listen for the following features:

➤ Balanced phrasing in two-, four- and eight-bar units

➤ Ternary form, in which all of the material derives from ideas in the first section:

> ➤ A: eight bars in G major

> ➤ B: four two-bar units that pass through E minor, C major, A minor and D major, followed by four bars that modulate from G major to V of E minor and four that return to G

> ➤ A: a repeat of the opening eight bars, extended into a coda with a varied repeat of the last half of the phrase

➤ The allocation of the melody to the bass at the start of the B section (accompanied by a contrapuntal idea in the wind).

Although these features help give the dance the required antique flavour, it doesn't use the most characteristic feature of the gavotte – phrases that begin with a two-crotchet anacrusis. Loewe's phrases begin with a single crotchet anacrusis, more in the style of a bourrée than a gavotte.

Stephen Sondheim opens *A Little Night Music* with an overture for voices instead of the more usual orchestral opening. This starts with a vocal warm-up from a group of five singers, whose role it will be to comment on the action throughout the musical, rather like the chorus in Classical Greek drama. They set the mood with quotations from some of the many waltz songs that dominate the show. The curtain then rises to the 'Night Waltz', an elegant and sophisticated dance during which the characters of the show are presented. Features to listen for here include:

➤ The melody for cor anglais (doubled by piccolo) with some slightly obtuse accompanying harmonies

➤ The response from the strings with clarinets in 3rds (and later with the strings playing in 3rds and octaves)

➤ Chromatic inflexions in the melodies

➤ The secondary theme on the flute and other instruments

➤ The re-entry of the singers, vocalising to 'la', near the end.

Exercise 16

1. To which part of a song does the term '32-bar song form' usually refer?

2. What is meant by a production number in a musical?

3. Where in a musical might you hear each of the following numbers: (i) the finale, (ii) incidental music, (iii) play-out music, (iv) an overture?

4. Choose two songs from the works that you have studied and use them to show how a composer adopts a specific musical style to suggest a certain period in history or a foreign location.

5. Compare two solo songs of a similar type by different composers from the works you have studied and present your findings to the rest of your A-level group. For example, you could choose two comic songs, two romantic ballads or two waltz songs.

6. Write a short account of the word-setting in one of the songs you have studied, showing how the composer has treated significant words and/or important rhymes.

7. Choose a musical that you studied which has a potpourri overture, and then write a paragraph to explain which numbers from the show appear in the overture and how they are treated. (Consider if they are shortened, expanded, transposed and so forth, and how they are linked.)

In section C of the listening paper there will be two essay questions on musicals 1940–1980, from which you must answer one. You will *not* have access to scores or recordings for this part of the exam.

Here are some questions for you to practise, but first make sure that you have read the tips about essay writing on pages 41–42.

Sample questions

(a) Choose and discuss two different songs from musicals that you feel successfully reflect the characters being portrayed.

(b) Discuss the role of the chorus in any one of the musicals that you have studied.

(c) Compare two scenes from the works that you have studied in which you feel that the music makes an especially dramatic impact.

(d) Examine the musical features of any one show of your choice that you regard as contributing most to its popular appeal.

(e) Compare and contrast two duets or vocal ensembles (but not choruses) from the works that you have studied.

(f) Choose two contrasting musical numbers intended for dancing on stage, and comment on how rhythm and instrumentation are used to bring out the character of the dance.

(g) Explain what is meant by '32-bar song form' and show how composers achieved variety in its use, drawing on examples from at least two different musicals in your answer.

(h) Examine two solo numbers from different musicals you have studied and, with reference to melody and harmony, discuss the way the two pieces are structured.

Section C: Area of Study 2c

British popular music from 1960 to the present day

There is a wide choice of music available for this Area of Study. When choosing your material, remember that you will have to answer an essay question which is likely to require analytical detail about the music itself rather than facts about the artists concerned. Try to include:

➤ A spread of styles, forms and artists from across the period

➤ A variety of emotional content in the music

➤ Songs that have potential for a detailed discussion about the ways in which elements such as melody, harmony, texture, instrumental technique and technology have been used

➤ Information about the context of the songs and matters such as the ways in which they make social comment.

The scope of this book cannot cover every type of popular music from the period, but this section includes discussion of five varied songs, one from each decade in the period, plus several additional examples, to indicate the kind of approach that you will need.

The 1960s

The world-famous group from Liverpool, the Beatles, were the leading band of the 1960s. Despite going their own ways in 1970, they were still ranked as the greatest artists of all time by *Rolling Stone* magazine in 2004.

'Love Me Do' was written in the late 1950s by band members Paul McCartney and John Lennon and was recorded in 1962 for release as the Beatles' first single. It was influenced by the American rhythm-and-blues style, evident in the simple harmonic pattern, blue notes in the melody and characteristic tone of the harmonica (mouth organ). The song has a clear structure:

Intro	8 bars	
Verse	13 bars	'Love, love me do ...'
Verse repeated	13 bars	'Love, love me do ...'
Middle 8 (or Bridge)	8 bars	'Someone to love ...'
Verse	13 bars	'Love, love me do ...'
Instrumental	12 bars	*(based on the bridge, not the verse)*
Verse	13 bars	'Love, love me do ...'
Coda (or Outro)	fade out	'Yeah, love me do ...'

The intro immediately sets the style. As well as the harmonica melody there is a classic rock beat (bass drum on 1 and 3, snare on 2 and 4, both with occasional added detail), and a straightforward chord pattern alternating between G (the tonic) and C. The melody could not suggest the blues sooner: not only is there the wailing harmonica (listen for the vibrato) but also the first note is the flattened 7th of the scale. The two-bar falling melody (*right*) at the start is a **hook** – a short melodic idea in a pop song designed to be instantly memorable. It comes three times in succession, followed by a brief cadential figure to complete the eight-bar introduction.

Paul McCartney and John Lennon are the two vocalists. McCartney also plays the bass guitar and Lennon also plays the harmonica (which explains why, when the harmonica is heard in the verses, there is only one vocal part). George Harrison plays guitar. Ringo Starr, who became the permanent drummer for the Beatles in 1962, features on the single version of 'Love Me Do', but a later recording, made with session drummer Andy White, was used when the song was included on compilation albums.

The verse maintains many of the same features: two-bar phrases and alternating chords of G and C, although this time the melodic shape is rising rather than falling. Note the syncopated ending to many of the phrases. During the first eight bars of the verse there is a second vocal part in homophony with the tune.

The harmony comes to rest on a chord of C major in bars 7–9 of the verse. After a moment's silence McCartney alone sings 'Love me do', with a prominent blue 3rd (B♭) at the start of the word 'do'. At this point, the harmonica (which has so far been silent in the verse) enters with the hook in counterpoint to the vocal solo.

The verse is repeated with the same lyrics, after which comes the **middle eight** (or **bridge**). It provides contrast because:

➢ All three primary triads of G major are now used (D, C and G), with the bright sound of the dominant chord (D major) making its first appearance at the start of this section

➢ The **harmonic rhythm** is different – at the start of the verse there was one chord per bar, but at the start of the bridge the chord of D lasts for two bars: verse | G | C | G | C |
                               bridge | D | D | C | G |

➢ The bridge consists of falling melodic phrases, whereas the verse contained rising melodic phrases

➢ The texture is different: in the first and third two-bar phrases there is only one voice, doubled by the harmonica, and when the second voice does join in (phrases two and four) it is in octaves with the other voice, not in harmony.

Another repetition of the verse, still with the same lyrics, leads to an **instrumental**, based on the bridge and featuring a harmonica solo. The passage is extended to 12 bars by adding four bars of G major harmony, after which the verse returns for a final time. The **outro** is based on material already heard.

The 1970s

The London-based rock group Pink Floyd achieved fame in the late 1960s for their combination of elaborate light shows with musical performance, something very in tune with the psychedelic craze of the period. A change of personnel in 1968 led to something of a change of direction, and their material became focused on various forms of alienation (madness, despair, death), which appealed to a generation growing up during the time of the Vietnam war and in an age when the Cold War between the USSR and the West seemed to pose an ever-present threat to mankind.

A detailed account of another famous pop album from the 1970s, *Who's Next* by The Who, is given in:

The Who: Who's Next in Focus by Julia Winterson. Rhinegold Publishing, 2007. ISBN 978-1-906178-12-3.

Their album *The Dark Side of the Moon*, released in 1973, became the fifth highest-selling album of all time and is one of the most famous examples of **progressive rock** – a style in which musicians sought to develop new structures for rock music, to incorporate novel ideas (such as the use of $\frac{7}{4}$ time in the track 'Money') and to explore unusual timbres by drawing on technological advances in recording and utilising the new synthesisers that were just starting to appear at this time.

The line-up on this famous album is:

➤ David Gilmour (vocals, guitars, VCS3)

➤ Nick Mason (percussion, tape effects)

➤ Richard Wright (keyboards, vocals, VCS3)

➤ Roger Waters (bass guitar, vocals, KCS3, tape effects)

The Dark Side of the Moon is a **concept album**, i.e. one where all the songs contribute to an overall theme, to make an artistic whole to be listened to complete, rather than just a collection of separate songs.

'Speak to Me' is the first track on this album and functions as a sort of overture. There is no traditional musical content in the first 70 seconds of this track. Instead there is a collage of sound effects, anticipating the tracks that follow. It starts with a heartbeat (later heard at the end of 'Eclipse'), followed by ticking clocks (referring to the song 'Time'), manic laughter (a reference to 'Brain Damage'), the sound of a cash register ('Money') and helicopter noises ('On the Run'). Layered over this are fragments of conversation about madness. A drone on B gradually emerges, which turns out to be the dominant of E minor, the key of the next track ('Breathe') which follows on seamlessly, its opening chord suggesting that music is the only release from the confused noises of life.

There are two eight-line verses in 'Breathe', set to the same music, preceded by an extended instrumental passage which goes once through the music of the verse. The tempo is quite slow (typical of Pink Floyd) and in four-time; the drummer plays even quavers, with the bass drum on the downbeat and the snare drum on beat 2 (and sometimes on beat 4 as well). Guitars and synthesizers are to the fore.

There are two distinct halves to the verses. The first four lines are based on the progression Em^9–A, while the last four lines are based on the more colourful progression C^{maj7}–Bm–F–G–Dm^7. The bass then moves chromatically up through D♯ to begin the next verse on the Em^9 chord. The harmony includes many 7ths, 9ths and suspensions, and its complexity is clearly much more jazz-influenced than the simple triadic harmony of the Beatles' 'Love me do'.

The 1980s

Elton John is one of the few real fixtures on the popular music scene of the last 40 years, and is the second most played artist on British radio (after George Michael). His 22nd studio album, *Sleeping with the Past*, appeared in 1989, from which the song 'Sacrifice' became his first solo number one single in the UK in 1990 (his many earlier successes being based more on albums than singles).

It was a timely boost, following some dark days in the middle of his career. It also marked a move in a new direction: the scoring is much more dependent on electronic sounds than his earlier music which is piano-based (he had studied piano at the Royal Academy of Music from the age of 11) and often supported by exciting arrangements for strings.

The VCS3 ('Voltage Controlled Studio' with three oscillators) was one of the earliest portable synthesisers. It had no keyboard and first appeared in 1969:

The idea of creating a collage by manipulating fundamentally non-musical sounds in this way originated with *musique concrète* in Paris in the late 1940s. Similar techniques had been used by the Beatles in their 1967 album, *Sgt. Pepper's Lonely Hearts Club Band*.

'Sacrifice' uses three keyboard players, bass guitar and drums. Elton John sings the solo part and there are some backing vocals. It is a ballad, with lyrics by Bernie Taupin, with whom Elton John had first collaborated in 1967. It uses a very tonal language and has a verse-and-chorus structure (in the following table, the key is shown as C major for simplicity, but on the recording it appears to be a little higher):

Intro	8 bars	| C | Em | F | F | (twice)	
Verse 1	16 bars	| C | F | Dm | G | (twice) | Am | F | G | G | (twice)	It's a human sign ... Into the boundary ...
Pre-chorus	8 bars	| C | F | Dm | G | (twice)	Cold, cold heart ...
Chorus	14 bars	| C | C | F | F | G | G | C | C | | C | C |Dm/C|Dm/C| Em |F G|	And it's no sacrifice ... But it's no sacrifice ...
Link	4 bars	Same chord progression as intro, but used just once here	
Verse 2	16 bars	Same music as verse 1, but new lyrics: Mutual misunderstanding after the fact ...	
Pre-chorus	8 bars	Repeat of pre-chorus with same lyrics	Cold, cold heart ...
Chorus	14 bars	Repeat of chorus with same lyrics	And it's no sacrifice ...
Link	4 bars	Repeat of link (slightly varied at the end)	
Verse 3	8 bars	Instrumental, based on the first eight bars only of the verse	
Pre-chorus	8 bars	Repeat of pre-chorus with same lyrics	Cold, cold heart ...
Chorus	14 bars	Repeat of chorus with same lyrics	And it's no sacrifice ...
Outro	Fade out	Last four bars of chorus, repeated to fade	

It's a hu - man — sign ——

when the scent of her lin - gers —

There are three features in particular to note in this song:

➢ The melodic ideas in the verse and pre-chorus are mainly based on the two short figures shown *left*: an arch shape and a simple rising semitone. In contrast, while the melody of the chorus is also fragmentary, the motifs are more varied and build into a longer and more shapely phrase.

➢ The chorus is also contrasted by a change in harmonic rhythm. There is mainly one chord per bar in the verse and pre-chorus, but in the chorus itself each chord lasts for two bars, giving greater stability and calmness, until the harmonic pace quickens before the cadence. Listen especially to bars 9–12 of the chorus, where the bass note C is at first consonant with the C major chord above it, but is then suspended to become a dissonance as the harmony moves to a chord of D minor.

➢ Listen carefully to the range of timbres produced by the various keyboards used in the song: many have an ethereal quality (resonant and sustained with little sense of attack at the start of the note) such as the string pad with which the song starts. However, later there are some more edgy timbres incorporated into the general wash of sound.

The 1990s

The Manchester-based rock group Oasis was founded by brothers Noel and Liam Gallagher in 1991. Many consider them to be the most significant band in the **Britpop** movement of the mid-1990s. After their third album, *Be Here Now*, had met with some critcism, Oasis responded by releasing a compilation album of songs in 1998 under the title *Masterplan*. Although claimed to consist of 'B-side' material, Noel Gallagher later admitted that there was 'a lot more inspired music on the B-sides than there is on *Be Here Now*.'

> Britpop was a mid-1990s style of rock music that was strongly influenced by British pop music of the 1960s and 1970s, featuring guitar-based bands that could perform songs live with simple chord progressions, verse-and-chorus forms, catchy melodies and lyrics about everyday life.

'Underneath the Sky', the second track on *Masterplan*, is written in a modal-sounding B minor. It opens with a short solo for lead guitar before the other guitars and drums join in. The song then unfolds in a familiar verse-and-chrous structure:

    Intro
        Verse 1
            Pre-chorus
                Chorus
        Verse 2
            Pre-chorus
                Chorus
        Verse 3 (instrumental)
            Pre-chorus
                Chorus
    Coda

The bass **riff** for the verse has an attractive asymmetry created by repeating a six-crotchet pattern in quadruple metre:

In contrast, the pattern for the chorus is more four-square: two beats of G, two of A and four of B minor. There is, however, a surprise near the end of the chorus when, instead of an expected modal cadence onto the tonic (A–Bm), there is an interrupted cadence: A–G♯ minor. In fact, it is a double surprise, since G♯ is outside the mode of the song up to this point. It launches a new pattern for the final bars of the chorus, G♯m–G♮–Bm–A, which is played three times, followed by G♮–F♯$^{\text{sus 4}}$–A. The delayed modal cadence is at last heard when the chord of A is followed by a chord of B minor at the start of the following verse.

Another surprise is the choice of piano as the melodic instrument for the short instrumental section. The last chorus is extended into a coda, at the end of which the harmonic rhythm slows down beneath repetitions of the final word ('again, again, again') to make a conclusion of some impact.

The 2000s

The London-based group Coldplay were formed in 1997. Their third album, *A Rush of Blood to the Head*, was written in the aftermath of the 9/11 terrorist attacks and was released the following year, receiving NME's Album of the Year Award for 2002. Several tracks

Coldplay's line-up consists of:

Chris Martin (vocals and piano)
Jonny Buckland (guitar)
Guy Berryman (bass guitar)
Will Champion (drums)

from the album became popular singles, including 'The Scientist', which has subsequently been sung by a number of other artists.

'The Scientist' is a piano-led ballad with the following structure:

Intro
    Verse 1
        Chorus
            Interlude
    Verse 2
        Chorus
        Instrumental
Coda

The intro is played by piano alone. The slow tempo and repeating straight quavers create a sad and hypnotic mood, reminiscent of music by some minimalist composers. This is further heightened by an unusual chord progression which starts on Dm^7 and ends on an unresolved suspension (Dm^7–$B\flat$–F–F^{sus2}). This is played twice before the vocals start, still accompanied solely by piano.

The vocal melody opens with the syncopated motif shown *left*, which is repeated and varied to form a four-bar phrase that is heard four times in the verses. The repetition, coupled with the minor chord at the start of phrases, conveys a sense of resignation.

Syncopated figures, but in a higher tessitura, also dominate the chorus, where there is a subtle change in the harmonic progression but little difference in mood or texture. A guitar eventually enters in the interlude, and then drums and bass for verse 2. Halfway through this verse another timbre, that of wordless backing vocals singing 'oo', is introduced. A tambourine is also used discreetly in the chorus that follows.

Coldplay underplay the instrumental section. The guitar is more prominent, but there is no spotlight on a big instrumental melody that might dilute the spell of the song. After a while, some wordless falsetto singing is introduced as the number moves towards its coda.

Other styles of British popular music

There are many other areas of popular music which you could choose to look at for this Area of Study. The following three songs might give you further ideas for material to use.

Indie rock

In practice, if an indie group or indie label becomes successful, their output is often bought out by one of the large record companies.

Indie rock ('independent rock') is a movement that developed in the 1980s among musicians who wanted to produce recordings independently of the major record labels, allowing them greater control over their music and careers. It is therefore something of an umbrella term, that covers a diverse range of music. However, many bands were guitar-based and some, such as the Stone Roses, were influential on the development of Britpop in the 1990s.

Razorlight is an Anglo-Swedish band formed in 2002 by London-born singer-songwriter Johnny Borrell. The two guitarists are both Swedish: Björn Ågren (lead guitar) and Carl Dalemo (bass guitar); the current line-up was completed when Andy Burrows joined as the band's drummer in 2004.

'Who Needs Love?' appeared on Razorlight's second album (rather confusingly called *Razorlight*), which entered the UK album chart at number one in July 2006. The song has a standard verse-and-chorus structure:

Intro
　Verse 1
　　Chorus
　Verse 2
　　Chorus
　Instrumental (based on the verses)
　Verse 3
Outro

The track is based on a limited harmonic palette. The introduction establishes the two main chords (A and F♯ minor; I and VI), alternating between them for four bars (one chord per bar). These chords are presented in simple fashion – triads in straight quavers, mid-range on the piano. A simple, clear drum pattern is used throughout (see *right*).

The verse uses the same chords as the introduction, in the same harmonic rhythm, before introducing chords IV and V. The melody of the song is confined to a compass of a major 6th (E–C♯). The same music is used twice in the complete verse, the extra line of lyrics in the second half of the verse calling for two extra bars. The full pattern for the verse is therefore:

Bars 1–2	Line 1 of lyrics	A / F♯m
Bars 3–4	Line 2 of lyrics	A / F♯m
Bars 5–8	Line 3 of lyrics	D / E / A / F♯m
Bars 9–10	Line 4 of lyrics	A / F♯m
Bars 11–12	Line 5 of lyrics	A / F♯m
Bars 13–16	Line 6 of lyrics	D / E / A / F♯m
Bars 17–18	Line 7 of lyrics	A / F♯m

The chorus has the same chord pattern as bars 1–8 of the verse, contrast being achieved firstly through lyrics with fewer syllables in lines 1 and 2 (four syllables rather than seven or eight) and through the simpler melody that this generates.

A development in the instrumentation occurs at the second verse with the introduction of the bass guitar. Notice how, in the example *below*, it emphasises the fifth of the triad in the chords of A and E. This creates a sense of forward movement towards the chorus, where more conventional root positions figure more prominently.

The instrumental solo after the second chorus is played on the lead guitar (Ågren) and is economic: just eight bars, following the basic chord pattern of the verse.

The final verse starts with the same lyrics as the first and includes the use of backing vocals. A change of lyrics generates an interesting moment on the line 'But I just can't give up without a fight, not I', where syncopation is used, and – as though to draw attention to it

– instruments leave the voice unaccompanied at the most intricate rhythmic moment:

But I just can't give up with-out a fight, not I

Ska
The origins of ska go back to Jamaica of the 1960s, where it was one of the precursors of reggae, although rather faster in tempo. Ska first came to attention in Britain with two hugely successful tracks recorded by Jamaican singers – Millie's 'My Boy Lollipop' (1964), followed in 1968 by Desmond Dekker's 'Israelites', a number one hit in the related but slower style known as rock steady.

However, both were regarded at the time as 'novelty numbers' and it was not until the success of such reggae stars as Bob Marley in the 1970s that West Indian styles became more widely known in Britain. A revival of interest in ska during the late 1970s led to British-born musicians producing their own interpretation of the style, combining the calypso and rhythm-and-blues roots of ska with the home-grown tradition of punk rock.

The Midlands-based group the Specials reflected these origins in its line-up for their chart-topping single 'Ghost Town', recorded in 1981. Jerry Dammers (keyboard player) brought together Jamaican guitarist Lynval Golding and singer Neville Staple, and the punk musicians Terry Hall (vocals) and Roddy Radiation Byers (guitar). Horace Panter (bass guitar) and John Bradbury (drums) were the other significant members of the band.

The song reflects many of the political issues of the day, particularly race-related violence and unemployment, and much of the music captures this rather bleak mood: there is no obvious verse-refrain structure and the mostly C minor based material becomes rather oppressive.

The relatively long intro opens with some electronically-generated timbres involving pitch-bending and wind-effect sounds. The first chord progression is a chain of six diminished 7th chords (with a chromatically rising top line) that create a scary sense of tension. This leads into the main chord pattern which establishes C minor as the tonic. The two main melodic ideas, shown *left*, are a motif that twists around the augmented 2nd at the top of the harmonic minor scale and a bass riff.

Active bass lines are a feature of ska and drums, as are chords on off-beat quavers. The drummer's emphasis of the backbeats (beats 2 and 4) demonstrates ska's close affinity with reggae. The opening melodic idea is answered by syncopated trumpet and trombone motifs (another element from Caribbean musical traditions) that lend a rather sardonic character. Synthesised timbres are also used near the end of the intro.

The lyrics are delivered in a heavy Jamaican accent, and the first and third lines are more spoken than sung. Line 4 imaginatively ends with an E major chord (in second inversion), offering a small sense of optimism. However, an instrumental interlude, very rooted in the tonic C minor and based on a descending chromatic scale, maintains the mood, with some backing vocals that have been given some extra reverb in the recording mix.

The interlude ends with a reprise of the diminished 7th chords and this suddenly arrives on a chord of D^7, marking the start of the one passage in the song in a brighter mood. The lyrics look back to 'the good old days' and to match this the key changes to G major. The chord pattern is V^7–I–V^7–I, one of several features that suggest the happy mood of calypso. Other elements adding to the good cheer are the energised bass line (hints of a walking bass here) and the flamboyant high trumpet line.

The happy memories do not last long: an A♭ chord takes us straight back to C minor and a return of the opening music. When the lyrics resume there are some extra layered lines (the song was recorded on eight tracks). Another instrumental interlude links to the outro, which starts with just drums and bass (a reminder of the role that rhythm and blues played in the origins of ska). Voices repeat the line 'This town is coming like a ghost town'. Electronic effects are evident here – the voices sound somewhat distant and there is a synthesised wind sound. For the third repetition the bass guitar stops and the drums are silenced just as the fourth repetition of the lyric begins. Finally, we are left with just the wind blowing.

Stadium rock

Composers have often been influenced by the places in which their works were first performed. Thus Gabrieli made use of the echo and antiphonal effects possible in St Mark's, Venice, Handel scored his *Fireworks Music* for a huge number of wind players because it was intended for outdoor performance, and Chopin was influenced by the intimate surroundings of the salons of Paris. In the same way, the growing confidence of the popular music industry to stage concerts at huge stadiums such as Wembley led to an idiom of rock music that suited live performance at such large-scale events.

Stadium rock grew out of such late-1970s styles as heavy metal, but with the harder edges toned-down to offer the mass appeal required for very large audiences. Big, infectious hooks are often used, as in Queen's 'We Will, We Will Rock You', that invite the audience to join in, and an anthem-like quality is also frequently evident. Performances of stadium rock typically often involve a lavish stage production, including lasers, smoke machines and very powerful amplification.

The iconic rock band Queen were formed in 1970 by Brian May (guitar), Freddie Mercury (vocals) and Roger Taylor (drums); bass player John Deacon joined the line-up a year later. But it was not until the mid 1970s that they became widely known, particularly with the release of their 1975 album *A Night at the Opera*, which includes one of their most famous tracks, 'Bohemian Rhapsody'.

In 1976 Queen gave a free concert in Hyde Park for upwards of 150,000 fans; 'Somebody to Love', which appeared on their album *A Day at the Races* at the end of that year, illustrates well how their music was written on a similar scale. Most striking is the way the musicians' voices are multitracked in order to create the aural illusion of a 100-strong Gospel choir. The album went to number one in the UK charts.

The intro of 'Somebody to Love' is for voices, with discreet piano backing, and, as in Gospel style, starts slowly and with a free approach to rhythm that includes several pauses. Starting from a tonic solo note of A♭, the choral parts fan out with melody and bass in contrary motion, a feature that occurs throughout the song. This gives a sense of confident expansiveness to the music appropriate for a big stage. In fact this choral material later becomes (in stricter tempo) the short refrain of the song.

some - bo - dy   to   love? _____

The last line of this refrain ('Can anybody find me somebody to love?') is particularly infectious, with a long, lingering note midway on 'me' and a final hook that Freddie Mercury decorates each time but always finishes conclusively on the tonic (the cadence figure at the end of the second refrain is shown *left*).

The verse has a strong melodic content, supported by an equally bold harmonic progression which makes frequent use of the bright sound of the 'dominant of the dominant' chord (B♭ major): the tonic key is A♭, so the dominant is E♭, and *its* dominant is B♭ – this type of chromatic chord is known as a **secondary dominant**.

After twice through the verse and refrain (with its straining to modulate in a dominant direction) a middle section follows which balances by starting in the subdominant (D♭ major). The chord progression here starts with a long D♭ chord and moves to G♭ major followed by G♭ minor. Chords of B♭ major and E♭ major then prepare for the return of the tonic key of A♭ major.

An instrumental solo for lead guitar (played by Brian May) follows, based on the chord pattern of the verse. The vocals re-enter for the refrain. Another sung verse is heard, but this time the music breaks off before the refrain and becomes suddenly quiet. The line 'Find me somebody to love' is then sung 11 times, starting **a capella** (unaccompanied) and in unison (in a bass register). This builds both in dynamic and texture, soon moving to octaves and then chordal homophony. Rhythmic clapping starts to build up, offering an infectious feature for audience participation. This leads to the final refrain and the most decorated version of the final hook, rhythmically protracted and in Mercury's falsetto register.

Rather than an outro with a fade-out, the song ends in a coda with a final cadence. This is built around several more repetitions of the 'Find me somebody to love' lyric before finishing resoundingly on the tonic chord.

Exercise 17

1. What musical features might you expect to hear in a rhythm-and-blues song?

2. What is meant by the term 'outro' in a pop song?

3. By what other name is a middle eight sometimes called?

4. What do you understand is meant by a concept album?

5. Explain what is meant by a hook and give an example of one from a song you know.

6. Write a short account of the word-setting in one of the songs you have studied, showing how the composer has treated significant words and phrases.

7. Which aspects of earlier pop music influenced the Britpop movement?

8. Choose a pop song that you particularly like and describe its main features to the rest of your A-level group. Show how the song is structured and point out any interesting motifs, rhythms, textures and chord progressions. Illustrate your talk by playing or singing relevant examples from the song.

In section C of the listening paper there will be two essay questions on British popular music from 1960 to the present day, from which you must answer one. You will *not* have access to scores or recordings for this part of the exam.

Here are some questions for you to practise, but first make sure that you have read the tips about essay writing on pages 41–42.

Sample questions

(a) Show how composers have achieved variety in the use of verse-and-chorus form by discussing the structures of at least two different songs from this period.

(b) Choose two contrasting pieces of popular music written *after* 1980 and show how harmony and tonality are used in each.

(c) Discuss the importance of the bass part in popular music, drawing on examples from at least two different songs.

(d) Compare one piece of popular music written *before* 1980 with another written *after* 1980, commenting on both differences and similarities.

(e) Discuss the ways in which the use of technology is an essential feature in two songs that you have studied.

(f) Examine the musical features of any *one* track of your choice that you regard as contributing to its popular appeal.

(g) Discuss the view that Britpop was pure nostalgia and added nothing new to the popular music of the 1990s.

(h) Write an essay about the variety of guitar writing in the music you have studied, drawing on examples from *at least three* different tracks.

Unit 2: Creating Musical Ideas

Composing

This is a coursework unit, the submission for which must be completed under supervision. AQA issues briefs for composing on the 1 November, from which you choose one. You then have 20 hours of supervised time in which to complete your work.

Note that the work you submit has to be completed at your school or college – you are not allowed to take it home or to submit material that has been downloaded from the internet. However, you should have sufficient time before starting on the brief to learn and practise your composing techniques and gain experience in your creative work. You can also continue researching and practising composing skills outside the 20 supervised hours, providing that you are not working on your actual exam submission. You should be aiming to learn new skills throughout the course to augment those that you used at GCSE.

The three briefs set by AQA are:

A   Compositional techniques: completing two set exercises

B   Free composition or pastiche: writing a three- to six-minute piece in one of four set genres

C   Arranging: making an arrangement of a set folk-song melody for voices, instruments or ICT.

There is an interesting range across these three briefs from the specific and prescribed, to the open-ended and free-ranging.

Brief A offers a very structured option. There are two tasks, and for each the material in the brief dictates in large measure what you need to do. Although there will be several potential right answers (as well as many wrong answers), the scope for original thinking is limited. This may appeal to students who prefer performing to composing and who might feel stressed by the challenge to create something original starting from a blank page. This brief may also be a good choice if you hope to study music at university, since it will prepare you for some of the skills required in traditional harmony and counterpoint courses.

Brief B is the opposite extreme. You will have to compose a piece that lasts between three and six minutes and that fits one of four very broad genres. Although there are aspects of your work that will be important in the examiner's assessment of your piece, this option gives you great scope to be individual in your creative work. This may appeal to students who enjoy improvisation and free composition, and who might feel constrained by the rather exacting technical requirements of the exercises in Brief A.

Brief C falls between these two extremes. AQA will set a single folk-song melody and your challenge is to write an arrangement of it. This option offers scope for imagination and creativity, but the given material will also help provide a structural framework for your ideas.

More detail about Brief A follows below. If you are choosing one of the other options, turn to page 92 for Brief B or page 95 for Brief C.

Brief A: Compositional techniques

You have to complete two tasks for Brief A. Each is marked out of 30, so they have equal weight:

> Harmonise a given 16-bar diatonic melody in four-part harmony

> Write two melodic lines to fit with a given passage of keyboard accompaniment.

Harmonisation of a 16-bar diatonic melody

Your task is to find a series of chords that fits the notes in the given melody. This is most likely to need one chord per crotchet beat, though longer note values may creep in at cadences and if the melody is in $\frac{3}{4}$ time.

The melody will be diatonic (i.e. it won't include chromatic notes), although it may modulate to a closely related key.

Your chords should be written for four parts (soprano, alto, tenor and bass) on two staves, as follows:

> Soprano part (given): treble stave, stems pointing up

> Alto part: treble stave, stems pointing down

> Tenor part: bass stave, stems pointing up

> Bass part: bass stave, stems pointing down.

Keep the two staves well apart, as it is important that the stems of the two inner parts don't get tangled up. All notes that sound simultaneously should be aligned vertically, except when two notes on the same stave are one step apart, when the lower of the two notes must be offset, as shown *right* at *(a)*. This example also shows at *(b)* how to write the same note for two parts on the same stave.

Given that triads comprise three different pitches but you are writing in four parts, it follows that one of the pitches must be **doubled** (i.e. occur twice) in each chord that you write. This is most likely to be the root of the chord, as shown at *(c)*, but it can be the 5th, as shown at *(d)*. Take care before doubling the 3rd of a chord: if it is a major triad, the 3rd should *not* normally be doubled. The 5th can be omitted if necessary – as at *(e)*, where the root is doubled in three of the four parts – but never omit the 3rd of a chord.

The key of the given melody should be clear. If in doubt, consider the key signature and then the final note. Almost certainly the final note (which is likely to be the tonic) will be harmonised by a tonic triad so that the piece sounds complete.

For a simple introduction to harmony for beginners, with tips and practice exercises, plus examples of both the tasks for Brief A, see:

Understanding Harmony by Hugh Benham. Rhinegold Publishing, 2008. ISBN 978-1-906178-34-5

Getting started

The terms soprano, alto, tenor and bass can also apply to instrumental lines in four-part writing. If you prefer to write for instruments you can, if you wish, use four staves, with one part on each stave.

If you consider the key signature and final note of the following four-bar melody, you should conclude that it is in G major:

This means that the six triads (and the dominant 7th) shown *left* will be your main source of chords to complete the harmonisation. When working your own exercises, begin by writing out a chord chart like this to use for reference. Note that in a major key, chords I, IV and V (the primary triads) are major triads and have been shown with upper case Roman numerals as a reminder, whereas chords ii, iii and vi (the secondary triads) are all minor triads.

	G	Am	Bm	C	D(7)	Em
					(C)	
	D	E	F♯	G	A	B
	B	C	D	E	F♯	G
	G	A	B	C	D	E
G major:	I	ii	iii	IV	V(7)	vi

Here is another four-bar melody. From the key signature alone you might think it is in C major, but the use of G♯ in the tune and the final note (A) should lead you to conclude that it is in A minor:

This means that the six triads (and the dominant 7th) shown *left* will be your main resource for completing the harmonisation. Note that in a minor key, chords i and iv are minor while V is usually major (and will require an accidental to sharpen the leading note); chord VI is major, as is chord III (in which the leading-note is *not* usually sharpened), but chord *ii* is a diminished triad.

	Am	Bdim	C	Dm	E(7)	F
					(D)	
	E	F	G	A	B	C
	C	D	E	F	G♯	A
	A	B	C	D	E	F
A minor:	i	ii	III	iv	V(7)	VI

Although you are more likely to use the primary triads in your harmonisation, the secondary triads are a useful way of making the end result sound more sophisticated.

When starting out, it is a good idea to work on the principle that a melody note on the beat should be present in the chord at that point. You can work out the possible choices by searching through your chord chart. For example, in the key of G major, the note G occurs in chords I, IV and vi and could therefore be harmonised by any of these triads. Which works best will depend on the context.

Consecutives In this type of harmony exercise it is considered an error if two parts move in parallel unisons, 5ths or octaves between adjacent chords. If this occurs, you will need to avoid the problem by laying the chords out in a different way or by changing one of them:

Consecutives can appear between *any* pair of parts, so check all six possible combinations (SA, ST, SB, AT, AB and TB). Problems with consecutives can be minimised if you write the bass in **contrary motion** to the melody as much as possible. It also helps to keep the tenor part high (close to or above middle C).

Inversions

Inversions (see page 10) can add variety to your harmonisation and help avoid consecutive 5ths and octaves involving the bass part. Bear in mind the following guidelines:

➤ Root-position triads are more likely to be used for opening chords, at the main cadences, and on strong downbeats

➤ First inversions may well be appropriate on weaker beats of the bar

➤ Be cautious with second inversions: a good rule of thumb is to use only the second inversion of the tonic chord, and then only as an approach a perfect cadence (i.e. Ic–V–I).

The following passage shows how inversions can add variety and prevent too many leaps in the bass part. Notice also how the use of chord Ic in the last bar avoids anticipating a root-position tonic chord before the very end of the passage:

Harmony in root position throughout:

I vi ii V I IV I IV I IV vi I V I

Harmony with both root-position chords and inversions:

I vi iib V I IVb Ib IV Ib iib vi Ic V I

Passing notes

You may feel that a series of crotchets and minims in every part lacks rhythmic interest. Passing notes can help prevent this. Look out for places in all parts (except the soprano, which must not be changed) where the notes leap a 3rd. In many cases you can insert a passing note to fill this gap. Listen carefully to the result – not all potential passing notes sound good, and they should not be used to join one phrase to the next. Also, check that your new note doesn't introduce consecutive 5ths or consecutive octaves. Our previous four bars of harmony might now be upgraded to this:

I vi iib V I IVb Ib IV Ib iib vi Ic V I

Passing notes may also be implied in the given soprano melody. For instance, the example *right* would sound better if the circled quavers are treated as passing notes, rather than harmonising each of them with a separate chord.

Vb I vi ii

Cadences

Traditional melodies are constructed from a series of phrases, often of two or four bars in length. Each phrase will end with a cadence: a pair of chords that acts like punctuation in the music (see pages 8–9). If you can harmonise the cadences successfully, not only will you be assured of having at least a quarter of the exercise correct, but the completed cadences will act like the dots in a 'join the dots' picture, making it easier to fill in the other chords. In fact, many people find it easier to complete the cadences first, and then work out the chords that best lead up to these cadence points.

Chord ii(b) often works well before a perfect cadence, but Ib, Ic or IV are other possibilities. Study and play the following examples, and then try to recreate each one in different keys:

The majority of cadences are likely to be perfect or imperfect. The example *above* also shows a plagal cadence. If you need to write an interrupted cadence, use vi instead of I in one of the perfect cadence patterns (and check very carefully for consecutive 5ths and octaves, since these will often arise in a V–vi progression).

Voice leading and spacing

Voice leading refers to the way in which the parts move from one note to the next. Try to avoid large leaps, especially in the two inner parts – aim for movement by step or, where possible, stay on the same note as the chord changes. There are usually wider leaps in the bass part, but avoid following a wide leap with another in the same direction.

Any part that has the leading note should normally rise to the tonic in the next chord, although leading notes may fall to the 5th of the tonic chord at cadences. Similarly, 7ths above the root of a chord should fall by step to the next note.

Avoid gaps of more than an octave between the soprano and alto, and between the alto and tenor parts. However, the gap between the tenor and bass parts can be more than an octave – see *(a), left*. Remember the advice to keep the tenor part high.

Also avoid parts crossing, as shown at *(b)*, where the alto is lower than the tenor, and avoid parts overlapping – as at *(c)*, where the bass is higher than the previous tenor note.

Modulation

Given that the melody in the brief will be 16 bars in length, there is a strong possibility that it will change key at some point. You should be prepared to modulate to the dominant, the subdominant or the relative minor (or the relative major, if the melody is in a minor key). If the music modulates, you should expect another modulation in order to return to the tonic before the end.

A change of key should be obvious if there are accidentals in the middle, but the modulation may simply be implied. For instance, in the following example, the melody comes to rest on D at the halfway point, in the bar marked with a bracket. A plagal cadence in G major would be possible here, but not very effective. The fact that the F♯ marked * doesn't act like a leading note of G major (it doesn't rise to the tonic) is a clue that the music has modulated to the dominant, and that a perfect cadence in D major would work well at this point:

If there *is* an accidental to indicate modulation, it is likely to be one of the following:

➤ Raised 4th degree: a modulation to the dominant. For example, in the key of F major, a B♮ would suggest a modulation to the dominant, C major. In the key of A minor, a D♯ would suggest a modulation to the dominant, E minor.

➤ Raised 5th degree: a modulation to the relative minor. For example, in the key of F major, a C♯ would suggest a modulation to the relative minor, D minor. In the key of E♭ major, a B♮ would suggest a modulation to the relative minor, C minor.

➤ Lowered 7th degree: if the key is major, a modulation to the subdominant. For example, in the key of C major, a B♭ would suggest a modulation to the subdominant, F major. In the key of G major, an F♮ would suggest a modulation to the sub-dominant, C major.

If the key is minor, a lowered 7th degree suggests a modulation to the relative major. For example, in the key of A minor, a G♮ would suggest a modulation to the relative major, C major. But note that an accidental is not always needed for this particular modulation. In the fragment *right* the note marked * is a G♮, even though there is no accidental in front of it.

> Remember that accidentals don't always indicate modulation – if the key of the melody is minor, they could just indicate the altered 6th and/or 7th degrees of the minor scale.

When you find that the melody you are harmonising has changed key, you may want to write out the six diatonic chords of the new key that are now available to you.

It can be a good idea to pre-empt the appearance of the new accidental in the melody by having the same accidental appear in one of the other three harmony parts a beat or two before, if you can fit it in.

Controlling texture: adding two melodic lines to a keyboard accompaniment

Getting started

In some ways this is the opposite process to the harmonisation exercise and it allows for more freedom and creativity in your work. You will have a complete harmonic progression in the given keyboard accompaniment, which will be up to 24 bars in length. Your task is to use and decorate notes from the chords to construct two attractive melodic parts that fit the accompaniment. They can be for any instruments you choose, or for voices, or for electronic sounds. You have full control over:

➤ The relationship between the two melodies

➤ The shape and rhythmic character of each melody

➤ The register(s) in which the melodies are played or sung

➤ The possible use of rests in the melodic lines.

Several of the points you learnt in the previous section are also relevant to this task:

➤ You may well want to use passing notes (and perhaps other forms of melodic decoration) to give your added parts greater fluency and melodic shape

➤ You should observe the principles of good voice leading so, for example, leading notes should rise to the tonic and 7ths should fall by step to the note below

➤ You should make sure that your melodies do not move in consecutive unisons, 5ths or octaves with the bass line of the accompaniment.

You will need to think how the two melodic parts relate to each other. Here are some ideas, but remember that the results will be more interesting if the relationship between the two parts changes at least once during the course of the piece rather than staying the same all the way through:

➤ One part could occasionally rest while the other continues, creating a **dialogue** (like a call and response) between the two. Rests are particularly important if you write for voices or wind instruments – performers need to be able to breathe!

➤ The two parts could be independent melodies that fit together in **counterpoint** as well as fitting with the accompaniment

➤ The two parts could share the same ideas in counterpoint by **imitating** each other

> If you use parallel intervals, keep to the ones suggested here. Passages for two solo instruments or voices in unison often don't work well because the differences in intonation are too obvious. Consecutive 2nds, 4ths, 5ths or 7ths should be entirely avoided.

➤ Both parts could have the same melody, perhaps in **parallel octaves, 3rds or 6ths** (see the note *left* about other intervals). Only do this for a few bars, as greater independence of the two parts is likely to gain more marks

➤ One part could sustain a long note while the other has the main melody, and then the pattern could be reversed

➤ One part could take the main melody while the other decorates it with faster notes.

Making use of two or three of these methods is a good idea, but don't try to fit all of them into 24 bars – the resulting chopping and changing would be too bewildering in such a short piece!

More on melodic decoration

We have already seen that melodies can be decorated with passing notes – notes that fill the gap between two chord notes that are a 3rd apart. There are several other types of melodic decoration. **Anticipations** and **appoggiaturas** were described on page 14 and another is the **auxiliary note** (shown *right*). This is similar to a passing note but, having moved up or down a step, it returns to the note on which it started. Although very simple, auxiliary notes are a wonderful way of giving life to a melody.

Good melodic writing

Selecting melody notes from the given chords is the easy part of this task. The key to success is in choosing notes that offer the potential to create motifs that you can repeat, vary and develop, so that your melodies have structure and direction, and don't simply sound random.

Techniques to bring a sense of style to your melodies include:

➢ Increasing the amount of stepwise movement by using passing notes, auxiliary notes, appoggiaturas and anticipations

➢ Making a feature (through reuse) of a particular leap

➢ Repeating a short but memorable rhythm

➢ Using short rests to energise the line.

Working an exercise

You may find it helpful to start by writing down the pitches of each new chord in the accompaniment, as shown above the staves in the example *below*. These are the notes from which you can create a skeleton melody. Don't attempt to use every possible note – just select one or two pitches from each chord, with an eye to creating useful patterns.

Study the given accompaniment carefully for cadence points and features such as sequences. For instance, the pattern in bar 3 is repeated in descending sequence in bar 4, and so notes have been selected to reflect the sequence in the flute part. Notice also how the melodic shape in bar 1 has been echoed in the shape of bar 5:

Through using the ideas in the bullet points *above*, this melodic skeleton could be fleshed out as follows:

Overall this achieves a much smoother melodic line, with mainly stepwise movement, although there are rising 6ths in bars 3 and 4, and an octave leap in bar 5 (notice how the melody *descends* after these large upward leaps to avoid sounding too angular). Notice the following points:

➤ Bar 1: the use of the quaver rest on the downbeat provides a lively start to the phrase; there is an accented passing note (C) on the second beat and semiquavers before the barline lead the way into bar 2

➤ Bar 2: the original arpeggio has been turned into a scalic figure by the use of a lower auxiliary (the note A) and passing notes; the final quaver provides an anacrusis to the next phrase and fills a gap where the accompaniment has a crotchet rest

➤ Bar 3: the first leap in the melody is highlighted by the use of syncopation; a sense of forward movement is generated with a passing note on G and a lower auxiliary on E

➤ Bar 4: a descending sequence of bar 3

➤ Bars 5–6: the rhythm of bars 1–2 is reused and the melodic contour is partially inverted. Notice how the octave leap takes the melody into the flute's bright upper register.

Counterpoint and imitation

In the example *opposite* a second melodic line has been added, using some of the techniques listed at the foot of page 88. Note the following points:

➤ Bars 1–2: the two woodwind parts have the same rhythm and melodic contour, and are mainly in parallel 3rds. This works well because the flute part starts on the mediant and doesn't go down as far as the lower tonic

➤ Bars 3–4: here the oboe is in free counterpoint with the flute, having semiquavers in the first half of the bar where the flute is least active. Notice that the oboe starts after the flute so the two instruments are clearly independent of each other. In bar 4 the oboe follows the same descending sequential pattern already established in the other parts

➤ Bars 5–6: there is real overlapping of phrases here. In bar 5 the oboe part is a continuation of the previous bar. A new idea begins in bar 6, halfway through the flute phrase

➤ Between the two instruments, there are seven quaver rests in six bars. This is helpful for wind players and, more significantly, gives real vitality to the music.

Here is a quite different working of the same exercise:

Features to note in this version include:

➤ Bars 1–2: the oboe imitates the flute two beats later – notice that the pitches have to be adapted in bar 2 to fit the harmony, although the oboe's rhythm is the same as that of the flute

➤ Bars 3–4: a new phrase in the flute is given a distinct character with some upward leaps and triplet quavers, both contrasting with the first phrase. It is imitated four beats later by the oboe

➤ Bars 5–6: the two melodic lines are more free here and they cadence together in bar 6. It might be the turn of the oboe to start in the next (imaginary) phrase

Overall, the character of this version is less energetic than the earlier version, having no semiquavers or syncopation. Rests again provide breathing spaces for the wind players and draw attention to the imitative entries.

Submitting your work

Your work for both tasks in this brief must be submitted as a score in staff notation with a recording on either CD or minidisc.

The scores must show **detailed performance directions**, such as the tempo, dynamics, articulation and phrasing. Make sure that the staves are labelled with the appropriate instrument or voice names at the start.

For your recordings, you can use acoustic instruments, voices, electronic sounds, or any combination of these.

In conclusion

There has only been room here for a general overview of some of the main points about harmony and counterpoint. For more detailed information, along with plenty of exercises for practice, you are recommended to consult a good book on harmony, such as the one listed on page 83.

Brief B: Free composition or pastiche

Outline

Because credit can be given for your grasp of elements such as melody and harmony, it would be inadvisable to write a piece solely for untuned percussion instruments.

Also, be cautious about choosing to write pastiche – it is difficult to do convincingly unless you are very familiar with all of the subtleties of the style you are imitating.

If you choose Brief B, your task is to compose one piece of music that lasts 3–6 minutes. It can be written in entirely your own style (but see *left*) or it can be a pastiche – a work in imitation of an existing style, such as a piano piece in the style of the early Romantic period, or a song in the style of the Beatles.

Whatever style you use, your piece must belong to one of the following genres:

➤ **Vocal music**: either accompanied or unaccompanied. If it is unaccompanied, you must write for at least two voices

➤ **Music for small ensemble**: you can write for any combination of two or more instruments

➤ **Electronic music**: any electronic sound sources are allowed. There must be a significant amount of your own original material if you decide to incorporate samples

➤ **Keyboard music**: any type of keyboard instrument is allowed, including mallet percussion instruments such as the xylophone, vibraphone or marimba. The piece can be for a single keyboard instrument or for a group of up to four keyboard instruments.

You have to submit both a recording of your piece and a score or annotation of some kind. The score must include full performing directions, including tempo, dynamics, articulation, phrasing and other marks of expression. If you are reluctant to provide a fully notated score, make sure your annotation has information about how you have controlled all musical elements within your piece. In particular, make sure that it gives detailed information about the structure of your composition.

There are so many aspects to a composition that it is very easy to overlook some of the points an examiner will be looking out for. These include:

Aspects to bear in mind

➢ Does the piece have musical character and a clear structure?

➢ Has the potential of the musical ideas been explored through their effective development?

➢ Is the tonality of the music well controlled?

➢ Does the harmonic language of the composition give character and direction to the music?

➢ Is there an imaginative use of tone colour and texture?

➢ Is the potential of each voice or instrument exploited in an idiomatic way?

➢ Is the score or annotation well marked up with performance detail?

Begin by planning the resources you will use. If the performance of the work requires other people, discuss the capabilities of their instruments or voices – what range of notes is possible, are some keys easier than others, how does the tone vary across the range, are some notes difficult to play loudly or quietly, are there any particular things that are difficult or impossible for the performer, such as fast passages in a low register or complex chords on a keyboard instrument or guitar?

Getting started

Consider if your composition will have a particular function, such as a piece for a celebration, a modern dance track or a song to be sung in church. Think about the mood(s) you wish to convey – calm and reflective, energetic and exciting, or perhaps a work that contrasts different moods? If it is vocal music, you will need to find some suitable words.

Once you have a clear idea of what you want to convey to your listeners, it will become easier to invent some initial ideas. You may be able to do that in your head, but many people find it easier to begin by improvising short ideas. Keep a note of everything that seems promising, either by jotting it down on manuscript paper, or by recording it or by simply memorising it.

Be careful not to spend too long on this initial stage. The most significant part of composing is what comes next. Build your opening ideas into longer sections and invent a few contrasting ideas. Then start planning an overall structure that will give you scope to develop your material. As you do so, work out where the main areas of contrast will occur (contrasts in dynamics, texture and key) and where the point(s) of climax will occur. How will the piece start? How will it end?

As more and more of the piece takes shape, remain analytical about how it is coming together. Sometimes, quite late in the process, you may realise that another instrument is needed, that a particular section could be developed further, or that a new linking passage is needed. Sometimes you may have to accept that the piece would be improved by deleting a passage.

It is worth remembering that the most common reasons for AS compositions receiving poor marks include:

➢ Lack of rhythmic interest (constant crotchets and minims)

➢ Lack of tonal variety (everything in the same key, with no modulations)

➢ Narrow vocal or instrumental ranges (parts that never exploit high and low registers)

➢ Lack of variety in texture (everyone playing throughout, with one part on the tune and other parts accompanying). Remember that even a solo piano piece can have many changes of texture (thick chords, two-part writing, melody in the bass with chords above, delicate arpeggios, an unaccompanied melody, passages with both hands in the treble or bass clef, and so forth)

➢ So many diverse ideas that the composition fails to gel – a piece of the required length doesn't really need more than two or three distinct ideas, but it *does* need to exploit and develop them in order to sound unified.

All of this means that you need to be self-critical and prepared to reject or modify work that you spot has not fulfilled its potential. Some people find it useful to reflect on the emotional journey created by their music – has it engaged the listener and kept them wanting more, right through to the end? Or is it too predictable (over-reliant on musical formulæ) or too confusing (many new features but too little development of the main ideas)?

Getting the right balance is part of the art of being a successful composer and is often harder than the relatively simple task of inventing a few simple musical ideas. Once you have resolved these questions, make a first draft of the whole piece. Play or sing it through, record it if possible, and listen critically for weaknesses.

Rewrite as necessary and add performance details to your latest draft. Produce copies for your performers and then run through it with them. Make further revisions as needed and then set to work on a final score of your piece for rehearsal, performance and recording. Remember that a final score needs to give the following information as accurately as possible:

➢ The notes to be played or sung

➢ When they should be played or sung

➢ How they should be played or sung.

You should therefore give as much detail as you can over tempo markings, performance directions and expression markings. Don't forget to label the staves with the names of the instrument(s) and/or voice part(s) required. Consider giving your piece a meaningful title – something descriptive, such as Reflections, Battle of the Robots or Brazilian Nights, can give a much better clue to your intentions than an abstract description such as Sonata or Trio. If you use music software to produce a score, choose a small stave size that won't waste paper and check that staves don't overlap and don't contain silly numbers of leger lines or accidentals because the wrong clef or wrong key signature has been used.

When submitting your work, remember that there are no marks for elaborate bindings or impressive artwork – the examiner will only be interested in the musical content, and will therefore welcome a submission that consists of a few simple sheets clipped together.

Brief C: Arranging

Outline

For Brief C AQA will set a folk song which you have to work into an arrangement lasting between 3 and 6 minutes. There are various formats in which this can be done:

➢ An arrangement for instruments or for unaccompanied voices

➢ An arrangement for one or more voices with an instrumental accompaniment

➢ An ICT project (which could include some live parts if you wish).

You have to submit both a recording of your piece and a score or annotation of some kind. The score must include full performing directions, including tempo, dynamics, articulation, phrasing and other marks of expression. If you are reluctant to provide a fully notated score, make sure your annotation has information about how you have controlled all musical elements within your piece. In particular, make sure that it gives detailed information about the structure of your arrangement.

Method

Although the basic melodic material for this project will have been set by AQA, the points listed at the top of page 93 apply equally to this task. Begin by trying out various ways of treating the melody:

➢ What tempo best suits the tune?

➢ Would a change of metre be effective?

➢ What key(s) should you use? Your choice will probably be influenced by the instruments or voices you decide to use

➢ Does the melody work in both major and minor modes?

➢ Does the tune work as a round?

➢ Would the melody sound good over (or under) a drone?

➢ What different harmonisations of the tune can you invent?

➢ Do the words suggest particular techniques you could use?

➢ What musical character do you want to convey?

Once you have considered these questions (and others of your own devising) carefully map out your arrangement. This should involve addressing the following issues for each section of your piece: the voices or instruments you are going to use, the way you might vary the texture, any changes of key, metre or tempo that you are going to incorporate, the dynamics of each verse, which voice or instrument will have the tune for each section.

A good arrangement will not just keep repeating the tune with differences in scoring or harmonies, but will explore the musical potential of the given material. For instance, you might take a fragment of the melody and develop it in various ways. In the following example, the first four notes of the melody are detached and then used in inversion and sequence in an arrangement for clarinet:

This type of motivic treatment works well in an instrumental arrangement but is difficult to achieve in a vocal arrangement because of the need for the words to make sense. But if you are writing for voices you could, for example, develop a contrapuntal treatment of the melody, with imitation between the parts:

Once you have established your main ideas, plan the overall shape of the arrangement. How will it start? How will it end? Where will the point(s) of climax occur? How and where will the contrasts occur? Will some sections be repeated, or perhaps given a varied repeat, in order to help provide structure to the finished work?

Now you can start writing the piece out in detail. Try it out in performance, however roughly, and be prepared to make changes as a result. Measure out the available 20 hours carefully – you don't want to be rushed towards the end, since you will need time to prepare the final version of the score and the recording.

Remember that a final score needs to give the following information as accurately as possible:

➢ The notes to be played or sung

➢ When they should be played or sung

➢ How they should be played or sung.

You should therefore give as much detail as you can over tempo markings, performance directions and expression markings. Don't forget to label the staves with the names of the instrument(s) and/or voice part(s) required. If you use music software to produce a score, choose a small stave size that won't waste paper and check that staves don't overlap and don't contain silly numbers of leger lines or accidentals because the wrong clef or wrong key signature has been used.

Unit 3: Interpreting Musical Ideas

You will be assessed on two performances which can be undertaken at any stage of your AS course before 15 May. Your submissions will be recorded and assessed by a teacher, before being sent to AQA for moderation. You will have to submit a copy of the score with the recording (if there is no score, you can submit a lead sheet, detailed guide or a commercial recording of the piece).

Your performances must come from **two different** categories in the following list:

➢ A solo instrumental performance

➢ A solo vocal performance

➢ A solo instrumental performance on a second instrument

➢ An ensemble performance

➢ A performance through technology using sequencing

➢ A performance through technology using multitracked or close microphone recording.

Live performing

Each performance should last between five and eight minutes. This can be achieved either through presenting one long piece or two or more shorter ones.

Instrumental, vocal and ensemble performing all require many of the same skills. There needs to be an accuracy in your realisation of the piece, a sense of communication with your audience, and sufficient expressive qualities in the performance to show an empathy for the musical character and style of the piece. In addition, in ensemble playing, there needs to be a good sense of synchronisation with your fellow musicians. Your part in the ensemble must not be doubled by anyone else – so you cannot offer skills such as singing in a choir or playing as a member of the cello section in an orchestra for this category.

All of these factors should be borne in mind when you choose the music you are going to perform – your teacher(s) will give you advice on what is suitable.

Difficulty levels

You may also want to consider the difficulty of the music. There are four marks available for the 'level of demand' of the music you offer, with the full four being awarded to music that is consistently of a grade 5 standard or over. However, there are 36 marks available for other aspects of the performance (accuracy, communication and interpretation).

It really is not worthwhile trying to scrape an extra mark or two by performing something that you can only just manage. Slips and hesitations will reduce your mark for accuracy and will impair the sense of communication and interpretation in your performance. In short, you will lose many more marks than the one or two to be gained through playing a difficult piece. An easier piece is usually a better and wiser choice.

In fact, a good rule of thumb is to offer a piece that you have already performed successfully to others – not one that you are currently still learning. Gaining experience in performing, rather than learning new pieces, is one of the best ways to prepare for this unit. Although some nerves are natural, and can help a musician concentrate and be more dynamic in performance, the confidence that comes from knowing you have performed the piece several times before is invaluable. If previous performances have gone well, you will enjoy giving another, and this will come across clearly to your audience (and earn you those valuable marks for communication).

Look out for every opportunity to try out your AS pieces in other concerts. Ask your family, friends and fellow students to listen to you playing the pieces: they can be very helpful in giving you encouragement and some friendly criticism over how your performance might be improved. If your performance requires the help of an accompanist, make sure you have practised well together before any performance, and enjoy the partnership that you will have in performing your pieces.

Finally, mastery of any instrument (and the singing voice) is a long and patient process, but a hugely worthwhile and satisfying one. At the start of your AS course you know that 30% of the marks will be awarded for your performing skills. If you are going to choose a live performing option, make sure that you have a regular practice routine: it is not a skill that can be left to the last moment.

Performing through technology

Sequencing project

The requirements for this option are as follows:

➤ The piece must be at least 32 bars long

➤ There must be at least four independent instrumental or vocal parts

➤ Any style is acceptable

➤ There should be evidence of some tempo control in music of a Classical style

➤ There should be some use of drum kit for music in a pop or jazz idiom

➤ All projects should include some dynamic variation

Your work will need to show the examiner that you can control pitch and rhythm accurately, that you have a good understanding of controlling the timbre, balance and panning aspects of each instrumental or vocal part, that you have shown good attention to shaping the expressive detail of the music and that a clear awareness of musical style emerges from your work.

Multi-track / Close microphone project

The requirements for this option are as follows:

➤ The piece must be at least 32 bars long

➤ There must be at least four parts

➤ You should use effects (delay, reverb, etc.) as appropriate

➤ In the final mix there should be evidence of panning/stereo.

Your work will need to show the examiner that you have achieved a good balance between parts, that you have catered for a wide dynamic range, that you have utilised panning techniques to separate sounds of similar frequencies, and that there is good quality recording across a wide range of frequencies.

You will need to submit both the initial recording and the final mix down (as well as a score or detailed notes about the piece).

Tips for both technology options

If you choose a technology-based option you will need to plan your work carefully. Ensuring that you have access to the technology you need, when you need it, will be very important. Remember, too, that any live performers involved in the recording will need time to learn their parts and rehearse together. Allow enough time to reschedule sessions in case performers are not ready or are absent when you you need them.

You will need to develop a good level of skill in using the equipment. Some people have a flair for using technology, but nothing beats being properly acquainted with the full capability of the kit you use. Working at a few practice projects in advance of the real AS task will be very valuable, and minimise the amount of time needed for consulting the instruction manual.

Above all, make sure you know how to save your work, and keep back-ups of everything you do.

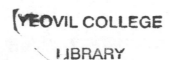